Why do we need think we need so muc
busy? In her wise, biblically minded, pr
through why we strive so hard to get "enougn in so many areas of our lives. And
then she leads us step by step back to the cross, the one place we will truly find
enough. Don't miss this perspective-changing study!

Afton Rorvik, author of *Storm Sisters: Friends through All Seasons*

Sharla's done it again. It's like she has a camera into my heart. She relates to
the hurts, challenges, and frustrations of everyday life. She opens God's Word
and teaches me to dig deeper and absorb more. A broken wanter, messed-up
desires, the God of sufficiency, enough for now . . . WOW! God fills every day
with enough for now. When I quit trying to store up an abundance for the future
and instead concentrate on the gifts God has given, my heart is full, my soul
content; it's enough! Thanks for once again speaking truth exactly where and
when I needed to hear it.

Teresa Nelson, LCMS Foundation

Whether you are reeling between the simplicity clause and the abundance dy-
namic, Sharla leads you thoughtfully through a powerful study that doesn't heap
platitudes or easy answers to our challenge of more and more. With transparent
stories highlighting her own struggles, Sharla opens the door of possibility to a
life that is "rich toward God." How does a God of sufficiency meet us with an eternity mind-set, in the margin, to be exceptional in the ordinary? This study offers
four levels of depth to move you gently along in a life of holy longing toward the
"freedom of living a life of trust."

Connie Denninger, Visual Faith Ministry

Thank you, Sharla Fritz, for writing a Bible study every one of us needs. We live
in a culture of endless shopping, constant eating, exhausting busyness, and too
many commitments. Collecting all this stuff isn't working for us though. We're
already stuffed too full of clutter, food, and stress. In this insightful new study,
your heart will be retuned to God's truth. Your completeness is in your Savior's
love. Through His sacrifice on the cross, you are already enough.

Christina Hergenrader, author of *Family Trees and Olive Branches*,
Love Rules, and *Last Summer at Eden*

Spot-on relevance for Christ followers living in a self-focused, broken world. This engaging study pokes at the heart of a tough issue. Sharla Fritz draws readers to self reflection and growth with her transparent, genuine style. Whether you gather your friends for a deep dive or go this experience alone, the solid biblical base will support you in the journey.

Linda Arnold, Women's Leadership Institute

In a world where we're continually told we need more (more stuff, status, self-confidence), it's no wonder we wrestle with having—and being—"enough." Enticed by promises that "more" will satisfy what's lacking in our lives, we attempt to fill a God-shaped hole with all kinds of things that don't fit, and we're left longing for more. After all, how much is enough? Can "more" really satisfy? Sharla speaks to our hearts as she tackles this timely topic with authenticity, truth, and grace!

Through engaging stories and compelling Scripture study, Sharla provides tools that help us discover what—and how much—is "enough." And this study doesn't stop there. Sharla provides engaging exercises that enable us to dig deeper into Scripture, apply the Word to our lives, and "cultivate enough" through unique group activities—to live out what we're learning together.

Learn what it looks like to rest in the God of sufficiency and His grace for you in Jesus. Receive His perfect provision, for He alone is the One who knows your needs more than you do; the One who truly satisfies your soul's longings—for now AND for eternity. Are you yearning to learn what satisfies? Our heavenly Father has the answer. We find "enough" in Him!

Deb Burma, author of *Joy*

Who doesn't struggle with feeling, having, or being enough? Sharla writes from an honest place about her own struggle for sufficiency. Her stories are relatable and engaging. There is room in the pages to engage with the text and guidance for group leaders to help digest the study's contents thoroughly. Sharla provides a very thoughtful and purposeful approach to the content, and many will be blessed by her attention to detail and storytelling! *Enough for Now* provides practical insights and biblical applications for our own journey toward sufficiency and points to the only one who can provide it—Jesus!

Darcy Paape, Women's Leadership Institute
and author of *Someone to Walk With*

enough
for
now

Unpacking
God's Sufficiency

A Bible Study by
SHARLA FRITZ

CONCORDIA PUBLISHING HOUSE • SAINT LOUIS

Dedication

To my family—one of this life's greatest blessings.
Thank you for helping me to live with enough for now.

Concordia
Publishing House

Founded in 1869 as the publishing arm of The Lutheran
Church—Missouri Synod, Concordia Publishing House gives
all glory to God for the blessing of 150 years of opportunities
to provide resources that are faithful to the Holy Scriptures
and the Lutheran Confessions.

Published by Concordia Publishing House
3558 S. Jefferson Ave., St. Louis, MO 63118-3968
1-800-325-3040 • cph.org

Manufactured in the United States of America

1 2 3 4 5 6 7 8 9 10   28 27 26 25 24 23 22 21 20 19

Table of Contents

INTRODUCTION

I scan the rows of shoes in my closet. I need just the right pair to go with my new outfit. I can choose from pumps, flats, wedges, sandals, and sneakers—a shoe for every occasion. I grab a pair of low-heeled sandals for walking the quaint main street of a nearby town with my husband. And on that walk is where I see them! A perfect pair of red pumps beckoning me from behind a plate glass window. My husband playfully pulls me past the store and says, "You have twenty-five pairs of shoes at home!" But suddenly fifty shoes are not enough.

I return home from lunch with a friend. This woman has walked with me through the struggles of raising kids, church life, and family health problems. Breathing a silent prayer of thanks for friends like her, I feel content—until I log on to Facebook and see pictures of a party I wasn't invited to. I'm grateful for the bond with my understanding friend. But now it doesn't seem like enough.

I successfully achieve a goal that has simmered on the back burner of my mind for years. After months and months of work, I celebrate the finished project. Excitement and relief fill my heart. Until I discover that someone else has done it better than me. Already grabbed the attention. Received the praise. My personal success is no longer enough.

What is enough? The word *enough* means "adequate for the want or need; sufficient or able to satisfy desire." Most of us have enough to meet our needs. But our desires? That's another story.

We live in a culture that constantly strives for more. We fill closets with more clothes and shoes. We stuff garages with more cars and tools, and when we run out of space, we rent storage units for our stuff. We cram our calendars with more activities. In order to get ahead, we take on more responsibilities and strategize more goals. Our bank account balance tells us we need more money, and social media tells us we need more followers.

Do we ever slow down to ask ourselves, "Do I really need more?" Could it be that the accumulation of "more" stuffs our closets but drains our energy? Does the amassing of activities fill our calendars but empty our souls? Perhaps the popularity of stories about the Amish way of life and blogs about minimalism demonstrate that we're sick of excess. We long for simplicity and yet we struggle with the question, what is enough?

As a Christian, I know I should be satisfied. I want to be like David and say, "The LORD is my shepherd; I shall not *want*" (Psalm 23:1, emphasis added). Or like Paul, who declared, "In any and every circumstance, I have learned the secret of facing plenty and hunger, abundance and need" (Philippians 4:12). But I continue to struggle. Even though I have done intense Bible study on contentment and have read oodles of books on the subject, satisfaction usually stands just out of reach. I still wrestle with "enough."

So, this book won't be telling you how to find "the secret of enough" in three easy steps. It isn't a memoir journaling my yearlong journey of selling all my stuff and moving into a 500-square-foot tiny home.

Instead, this volume chronicles my journey to the God of sufficiency. It tells how I learned that our insatiable desire for enough can drive us to God instead of propelling us toward more money, more stuff, more activity. It asks, "What is enough?" and helps us go to the Father for the right answer.

We each come to this search for enough from different situations. Some of you may be experiencing lean years—perhaps most months have more days than funds. Others of you may have plenty—at least plenty of stuff in your closets, basements, and garages. I have been in both situations and know that in both scenarios, we can still strain and strive for more.

Throughout this book, we will study Jesus' parable of the rich fool—a man who had so much more than enough that he built bigger barns to hold the overflowing excess. Like most of us, he based his happiness on having an ample supply. But Jesus taught that we can't find the secret of true riches by storing goods. We won't find security through accumulation.

This book is not meant to make you feel guilty about how much you own or don't own. Instead, it explores what God has to say on the topic of enough. It contains a set of tools to help you discover how much is enough for you. And it shines a light on a path to the God of sufficiency, who longs to satisfy our souls with Himself so we can confidently say, "I have enough— for now."

USING THIS BOOK

Each chapter of *Enough for Now* explores the concept of "enough" in a different area: money, stuff, food, relationships, time, and self-image. These are not easy topics—don't be surprised if your ideas about them are challenged. But even while you examine these concepts, the book will encourage you to focus on the God of sufficiency and His grace.

You may choose to explore the idea of "enough" by reading the book straight through. Each chapter includes
- memory verses;
- historical information about life in Bible times;
- questions for reflection and discussion;
- prayer prompts; and
- practical ideas for exercising "enough."

In addition to reading about "enough," I hope you will also take time to go deeper into the subject by engaging in the Bible study questions in the Study Guide beginning on page 147. These questions will help you to
- reflect on the reading;
- dig into Scripture;
- apply the lessons to your life; and
- cultivate "enough" through creative projects.

I encourage you to gather a few others to join you on this journey to "enough." Sharing the struggle to find contentment in a broken world will help your group draw closer to God and to one another. The study is designed to be completed in eight weeks, but if your meeting time is short or you simply want to take the journey more slowly, you may want to take two weeks for every chapter. In that case, you could complete the reading, answer the questions contained within the reading, and respond to the "Reflect on the Reading" questions in the Study Guide one week, then complete the "Dig into Scripture," "Apply the Word to Your Life," and "Cultivate

Enough" sections the next week. The "Cultivate Enough" projects may be especially enjoyable to complete as a group.

As you study, remember to

- begin with prayer;
- rely on Scripture to guide your discussions; and
- keep what is shared confidential unless you are given permission to share outside the group.

May the Lord bless you as you find "enough" in Him.

CHAPTER 1

WHAT IS ENOUGH?

Memory Verse:
Fear not, little flock, for it is your Father's good
pleasure to give you the kingdom. Luke 12:32

Not long ago, a local charity called and asked if I had any clothing or household goods I would like to donate. Of course I did.

In fact, I had just finished reorganizing my bookshelves, closets, and cabinets. On the day of the charity pickup, I set out four large boxes of books, two boxes of CDs and vinyl records (yes, I still had some of the old-school technology), and five garbage bags of out-of-date clothes.

I sent these things to a new home with joy, but there was a depressing aspect to this process. Even after getting rid of all those boxes of books, CDs, and clothes, my house didn't look much different. My closets still bulged with clothes. My bookshelves still held hundreds of books.

Clearly, if all my storage spaces still swelled with possessions—even after giving away a hundred pounds of stuff—I had too much. Why had I felt I needed more when I already had plenty? Why had my husband's wisecrack limiting me to no more than a hundred sweaters and fifty shoes struck me as a challenge instead of a warning? Why did I search for more?

The Problem of Enough

What is enough? The human race has always struggled with finding equilibrium between "not enough" and "too much." Satan, the world, and our own human nature continually make us yearn for more.

It all started back in the Garden of Eden. Adam and Eve had everything they could want: delicious food, rewarding work without any problems, delightful weather. They didn't need anything. And yet, Satan knew how to tempt them—to make them think they didn't have enough.

God had given Adam and Eve permission to eat from any tree in the garden—except one. He told them if they ate from the tree of the knowledge of good and evil, they would die (Genesis 2:16–17). Satan, however, tried to convince them otherwise. He said, "You will not surely die. For God knows that when you eat of it your eyes will be opened, and you will be like God, knowing good and evil" (Genesis 3:4–5). He insinuated that God was holding out on them. He tempted the first couple to want more—to be like God. Suddenly all the Creator had given seemed insufficient.

Satan continues to tempt us with the idea of more. He tries to tell us God is withholding His best from us. He whispers that what we currently have couldn't possibly be enough.

Exercising Enough

Take a minute to think about where you struggle with "enough." In which of these areas do you feel the greatest deficit?

Money _____

Stuff _____

Food _____

Relationships _____

Time _____

Yourself _____

What do you hope to gain from this book?

Satan isn't the only one. The world constantly bombards us with the message that what we have is insufficient. Television commercials tell us we deserve a luxury car. Internet ads inform us we need a week in Bermuda. Every roadside billboard, every gas pump video, every glossy magazine ad screams, "More!"

Our own human nature continually wages war against "enough." When I was growing up, the Frito-Lay commercial that interrupted my favorite television shows told me, "No one can eat just one." And it was true—one potato chip was never enough. I always wanted another—and another—and another.

This insatiable desire for more doesn't stop with salty snacks. I'm convinced that ever since Adam and Eve gave in to an appetite for forbidden fruit and a thirst to be like God, we have been stuck with broken "wanters." The part of us that hungers and thirsts and desires developed serious defects in the fall. Now, I possess a wanter that can make me crave a huge slice of chocolate cheesecake even after

> The human race has always struggled with finding equilibrium between "not enough" and "too much."

I've had soup, salad, and an enormous platter of chicken marsala. A wanter that can make me long for those adorable red pumps in the shoe store window even though I have twenty-five pairs of shoes in the closet. Our broken wanters prevent us from attaining enough.

In fact, our wanters are so broken that we sometimes have difficulty discerning our true desires. Because of widespread damaged wanters, a new profession has sprung up. For only two hundred dollars an hour, you can hire a "wantologist"—someone who will help you distinguish what you really want from what you only *think* you want. For instance, you might go to a wantology session with a wish for a promotion at work and leave with the realization that what you *really* want is to quit your job.[1] Because of our broken wanters, we don't know what will actually satisfy our souls. So, we continually search for the next bauble, the next promotion, the next relationship that promises happiness.

Even more serious, our broken wanters compel us to yearn for wrong things. Our damaged desire factories make us crave rocky road ice cream instead of broccoli. Sleep on Sunday mornings seems more appealing than worshiping with our brothers and sisters in Christ. Because of our sinful nature, we don't gravitate toward the wholesome or the virtuous. We continually want more than what God has deemed good.

On our own, we are incapable of achieving enough.

HOW HAVE YOU SEEN EVIDENCE OF A BROKEN WANTER IN YOURSELF?
CAN YOU GIVE AN EXAMPLE?

_____

_____

_____

_____

The Rich Man and Enough

Jesus knew about our broken wanters. He saw our tendency toward greed and covetousness. He understood our constant drift toward excess and overindulgence. In Luke 12, He told a story about a rich man who had a problem with enough.

> The land of a rich man produced plentifully, and he thought to himself, "What shall I do, for I have nowhere to store my crops?" And he said, "I will do this: I will tear down my barns and build larger ones, and there I will store all my grain and my goods. And I will say to my soul, 'Soul, you have ample goods laid up for many years; relax, eat, drink, be merry.'" But God said to him, "Fool! This night your soul is required of you, and the things you have prepared, whose will they be?" So is the one who lays up treasure for himself and is not rich toward God. (Luke 12:16–21)

Clearly, this man had enough to start with. He had wealth. The Greek word for "land" in verse 16 is *chora*, which is usually translated as "country" or "region." This man owned a huge estate. He already had barns—barns more than adequate for a well-to-do life.

But when his land produced a bumper crop, his first reaction was not thankfulness. He didn't praise God for the abundance. Instead, the reality of plenty made him anxious. He worried, "What shall I do?" You can almost see him wringing his hands and pacing the floor.

The rich man came up with a solution. He would stockpile the extra food. He would store additional supplies. And he told his *soul* that when he had more, he would be happy.

FARMING IN ISRAEL

Farmers plowed and sowed seed during the first part of the rainy season—October or November. Heavier rains, which watered the crops, usually came in December and continued through March or April. Harvest time varied with the topography of the land. People in the lowlands began harvesting at the end of April, while farmers in the hills brought in their crops in May or early June. Grain was harvested with a sickle and bound into sheaves. These sheaves were then taken to the threshing floor to dry. When dry, the farmer used animals or simple machines to thresh the grain, separating the grain from the straw and chaff. Next, he winnowed the grain by tossing it up into the air and letting the lighter chaff blow away, while the good grain settled back on the threshing floor. Finally, the grain was stored in barns.[2]

Two thousand years later, this story still rings true. Jesus could have inserted my name in this story. I don't have any barns or silos in my backyard, but I have had the same thoughts. Even though God has never let me go hungry, even though I've always had enough money to pay the bills, I have reasoned, "If I only had more, then I would be satisfied."

So how can we "find enough" in a world that constantly tells us we need more?

Desire and Disordered Loves

The first step in finding enough is acknowledging our broken wanters and the serious consequences of our messed-up desires. When Jesus told the parable of the rich fool, He began with a caution to His listeners:

> Take care, and be on your guard against all covetousness, for one's life does not consist in the abundance of his possessions.
> (Luke 12:15)

Jesus warns us we need to post a guard, be on the defensive. The Greek word is *phylasso*, which means "to guard against something for our own safety." And what are we to guard against? Covetousness. This Greek word means "the greedy desire to have more."

Jesus is saying, "Greed is a serious problem. So, beware. Watch out. Be very wary and careful. There is danger in always wanting more." Why is that? Jesus explains we can't base the good life on the abundance of possessions. Although car manufacturers and clothes designers want us to think our happiness depends on buying their products, genuine and full life does not consist of what we keep in our garages or closets. Society may define us by the size of our house or the name on our handbag, but thankfully Jesus does not. Instead, He warns that if we believe the myth that our lives will be better when we have more, we will never find satisfaction.

> We get in trouble when we look for "enough" in other places besides God.

It isn't necessarily wrong to have yearnings and desires. It isn't sinful to want to fill the emptiness inside. King David tells us God hears our desires; He bends down to hear our frantic prayers (Psalm 10:17). Jesus promises, "Ask, and it will be given to you; seek, and you will find; knock, and it will be opened to you. For everyone who asks receives, and the one who seeks finds, and to the one who knocks it will be opened" (Matthew 7:7–8). He invites us to ask for the things we want, to seek out our desires, to knock on doors yet unopened.

The problem comes when we want the wrong things or try to get what we want in the wrong way. Augustine, the fourth-century Bishop of Hippo, called these "disordered loves" or "corrupted longings."[3] Martin Luther warned against wanting something so much that we are willing to scheme to obtain it or get it in a way that only appears right.[4]

> Jesus warns that if we believe the myth that our lives will be better when we have more, we will never find satisfaction.

Difficulty arises when we chase the things the world holds out as the solution to our hunger, thirst, or passion—but they don't truly satisfy. Augustine wrote, "Love longs for some object to be, loves to rest itself in the thing beloved. But in things there is no enduring place to lie. They don't last. They run away."[5] Like the rich man in Jesus' parable, we think we can rest when we have stored up the object of our desire, but all earthly things eventually melt away like an ice pop on a hot summer day.

We get in trouble when we look for "enough" in other places besides God—when we search for adequacy by trying to fill our bank accounts, closets, and calendars. When we search for satisfaction in having a perfect family or a successful career. Difficulty comes when our wanting drives us anywhere but to deeper trust in God. In her book *Teach Us to Want,* author Jen Pollock Michel writes about the relationship between desire and trust:

> And here is how desire becomes corrupt: wanting derails into selfishness, greed, and demanding ingratitude when we've failed to recognize and receive the good that God has already given. Trust is at the center of holy desire: trust that God is good and wills good for his people. We trust in asking; we trust in receiving. Holy trust believes that whatever God chooses to give is enough.[6]

Let's begin this journey to "enough" by confessing our disordered desires. Michel writes, "Admitting the doctrine of sin is critical to any faithful conversation about desire."[7] Let's ask ourselves, "What wrong things have I craved? What good things have I wanted enough to obtain them wrongly? When have I abandoned holy trust, which accepts what God gives as enough?" As we take an honest inventory of our wants and wishes and repent of any sinful attempts to find "enough," we can receive forgiveness from Jesus, who paid the price for all our sin.

═══ COVETING ═══

This sin of covetousness is listed in the Ten Commandments:

You shall not covet your neighbor's house; you shall not covet your neighbor's wife, or his male servant, or his female servant, or his ox, or his donkey, or anything that is your neighbor's. (Exodus 20:17)

In the Small Catechism, Luther said this of the Ninth and Tenth Commandments:

We should fear and love God so that we do not scheme to get our neighbor's inheritance or house, or get it in a way which only appears right, but help and be of service to him in keeping it.

We should fear and love God so that we do not entice or force away our neighbor's wife, workers, or animals, or turn them against him, but urge them to stay and do their duty.

Prayer Prompt

Journal a prayer, confessing your disordered loves. What wrong thing have you wanted? Or what good thing have you attempted to get in a wrong way? Repent and receive Christ's forgiveness because of His sacrifice for you.

_____

_____

_____

_____

_____

The God of Sufficiency

After we have examined our broken wanters and received forgiveness for our missteps in the journey of desire, we take the next step in finding satisfaction and fulfillment by going to the right source—the God of sufficiency.

> [Jesus] is the very source of life and goodness, who fills us with joyful satisfaction through the Gospel.[8]

After Jesus finished the parable of the rich man, He went on to reassure His listeners about God's constant care:

And He said to His disciples, "Therefore I tell you, do not be anxious about your life, what you will eat, nor about your body, what you will put on. For life is more than food, and the body more than clothing. Consider the ravens: they neither sow nor reap, they have neither storehouse nor barn, and yet God feeds them. Of how much more value are you than the birds! And which of you by being anxious can add a single hour to his span of life? If then you are not able to do as small a thing as that, why are you anxious about the rest? Consider the lilies, how they grow: they neither toil nor spin, yet I tell you, even Solomon in all his glory was not arrayed like one of these. But if God so clothes the grass, which is alive in the field today, and tomorrow is thrown into the oven, how much more will He clothe you, O you of little faith!

And do not seek what you are to eat and what you are to drink, nor be worried. For all the nations of the world seek after these things, and your Father knows that you need them. Instead, seek His kingdom, and these things will be added to you.

"Fear not, little flock, for it is your Father's good pleasure to give you the kingdom." (Luke 12:22–32)

Jesus reminded His followers they didn't need to worry about food or clothing because the Father promised to look after their needs. Just as God cared for the grass waving in the fields and birds nesting in the trees, He would provide for them too.

Jesus tells all of us, "Look, you don't have to be like the rest of the world, chasing after things in the hope that possessions or positions will fill the emptiness inside. Live in trust that I know what you need. You are a part of My flock; you are following Me. But like sheep, you don't know what you need as well as your Shepherd does. Remember, your Father is a loving parent who takes great happiness in giving you the kingdom."

Exercising Enough

Scripture Reminds Us of God's Loving Concern for Us

[Cast] all your anxieties on Him, because He cares for you. (1 Peter 5:7)

How have you seen God's care for you in the past week?

_____

_____

_____

_____

_____

_____

_____

_____

_____

Our heavenly Father must be saddened when we try to meet our needs with our own power. Perhaps He shakes His head when we strive and struggle to obtain the bigger house or the more important job. Satan continually attempts to get us to view God as a miser who reluctantly gives out good things; to see the Lord as haphazard as the lottery when it comes to doling out blessings; or to believe we need to work extra hard to earn them. God wants us to view Him not as the Big Bad Guy in the sky holding out on us, but as the God of sufficiency.

God makes us capable of longing so we come to Him to fill those longings.

God makes us capable of longing so we come to Him to fill those longings. He makes us yearn for enough so we learn to trust Him for all we need and desire. Jesus said, "But if God so clothes the grass, which is alive in the field today, and tomorrow is thrown into the oven, how much more will He clothe you, O you of little faith!" (Luke 12:28). He reproaches our puny faith. But He also invites us to have confidence in the Father who dresses even transitory grass in beautiful colors and feeds tiny, insignificant birds.

Our journey toward "enough" can lead us down roads that end in frustration, disappointment, and sin. Often this happens. But we don't have to take those paths. Our desires can become routes to spiritual growth. They can lead to deeper faith in God.

Prayer Prompt

Galatians 5:16 says, "But I say, walk by the Spirit, and you will not gratify the desires of the flesh." As we walk hand in hand with the Spirit, He can change our desires. Write out a prayer asking the Holy Spirit to be your Divine Wantologist. Invite Him to search through all your wishes and yearnings. Ask Him to give you holy desires that will fill your heart with joy.

Psalm 37:4–5 says, "Delight yourself in the LORD, and He will give you the desires of your heart. Commit your way to the LORD; trust in Him, and He will act."

God "will give you the desires of your heart." I used to think this phrase meant God would grant me money, success—and cute shoes. But the true meaning is more like "Find your happiness in the Lord, and He will give you true desires." Better than any other wantologist, the Holy Spirit can help you sort out your longings and give you yearnings for what will truly satisfy. He can fix our broken wanters.

God invites us to commit our ways to Him. When I commit something, I entrust it to someone else. If I commit my desire to the Lord, I make Him the caretaker of my wish. I give Him the authorization to satisfy the need, now or later—to fulfill the desire immediately, or never. Not that He needs my authorization, of course. His will is always accomplished. But I free myself from the agonizing quest for "enough" if I leave it in His hands. Hear what Augustine beautifully declares:

> Weaned from all passing fancies, let my soul praise You, O God, Creator of all. You did not allow my soul to remain attached to corruptible things with the glue of love, attached to what my senses find pleasing. For things we are attached to go where they will, then they cease, leaving the lover torn with corrupted longings.[9]

When I desperately want something, I can do what comes naturally— attempt to get what I want on my own, consult the experts, read a dozen self-help books, and work hard. Or I can bring my desire to God. Bravely lay it on the altar. Surrender it to Him.

As I lay it on the altar, I am saying, "Lord, here is what I want. Here is what I feel I need to have enough. This ache in my soul doesn't seem to go away. But I give it to You, Lord. Do with it what You want. Of course, I prefer You would fulfill this desire (and quickly, if You please!), but if You decide that is not what is best, I trust Your plan. Fulfill the desire. Or remove it. Or reshape it. Thy will be done."

Author Caryn Dahlstrand Rivadeneira calls this kind of prayer "living dead." In her book *Grumble Hallelujah,* she writes:

> If we can trust God enough, we can start loving the life he has for us. We just have to be willing to live it dead. Because when we live it dead,

when we toss everything back to God and allow him to resurrect what he wants in our lives, we get to live in the freedom and pleasure of knowing that what we long for has been placed there by God.[10]

Fling all your desires into God's lap and trust He will grant only what is good for you. Rely on the One who knows your longings and will give you the best for your eternal happiness.

Let's find "enough" not in the number of sweaters we own (although they are some of my favorite items to accumulate and store), but in the sufficiency of God. As we bring all our desires to Him and lay them at His feet, we learn to trust that He knows how to satisfy our longings. Maybe not in the way we envisioned, but in the best way possible.

WHAT IS YOUR BIGGEST TAKEAWAY FROM THIS CHAPTER?

O GOD OF SUFFICIENCY,

I admit that I have believed the myth that my life would be better if I just had a little more—a little more money, a little more popularity, a little more recognition. I have wanted wrong things and have pursued good things in wrong ways. I have looked for contentment in what the world offers instead of in You, and I have been sorely disappointed.

Thank You for reminding me that You are the God of sufficiency. You are the good Father who sees my needs. You tell me You are pleased to give me the kingdom— more than I can imagine. I am overwhelmed when I think of all Jesus went through so that I could have a relationship with You. You fill my soul with joy and peace.

Help me to trust You with all my desires. Because I know Your true nature of goodness, this should be easy, but sometimes I doubt.

Enable me to lay all of my longings on Your altar with the faith that You will satisfy them in the best way possible. In Jesus' name. Amen.

CHAPTER 2

ENOUGH MONEY

Memory Verse:
For where your treasure is, there
will your heart be also. Luke 12:34

I opened the refrigerator and there it sat. On the top shelf quivered a large maroon cow's liver—inside a bright aqua bowl.

You might ask, "What was a cow's liver doing in your refrigerator?"

The short answer is "Thawing." The long answer requires a bit of a story.

My husband and I married while still in school. John had finished his bachelor's degree and one year of seminary. I was still working on my bachelor's degree. My sweet husband graciously offered to take a one-year break from the seminary and work while I finished my degree. Then we would switch, and I would work while he finished his master of divinity degree.

John found a job with an insurance company in my college town. The company assured him he could start after we returned from our honeymoon. However, after we unpacked our bags and moved our wedding gifts into our new apartment, the insurance company reneged on the deal.

Thankfully, God provided new work. A professor at the seminary commissioned John to do a research project on deaf ministry in America. Two area churches hired my husband as an unofficial vicar. These jobs were much better suited to John's talents and to his long-term goals, but they did not pay as well as the insurance job. We had enough funds to live. But just barely.

To save money, we ate liver. I know. Eww. But at that time, experts promoted it as a healthy source of iron. And it was inexpensive—you could get little orange cartons of sliced liver for 39 cents a pound. My mother-in-law's recipe—with tomato sauce, green peppers, and rice—made it almost palatable. And so, liver became one of our go-to meals.

One evening we searched the aisles of Link Brothers Fine Foods, looking for some meat we could afford, when we spied a large white box labeled "Beef Liver." The price was a steal: 32 cents a pound! Seven pounds of liver . . . *There must be a lot of little orange containers of liver in the box*, we thought. Well, we could eat some this week and store the rest in the freezer. So, we purchased the big, plastic-wrapped cardboard box of liver.

When we opened the box at home, no nice little containers of sliced meat greeted us. Instead one large, whole, frozen beef liver filled the box. Now what?

To tackle this hunk of meat, we decided to let it thaw in the refrigerator and then cut it into portions. We pulled out the only bowl we had large enough for this purpose—an aqua plastic wash basin we got from a friend who worked in a plastics factory. For two days, every time we opened the refrigerator, the sight of a maroon organ sitting in an aqua bowl greeted us.

NAME SOME OF YOUR STRUGGLES WITH MONEY.

_____

_____

_____

_____

_____

We laugh now. Our life as newlyweds had its challenges. Money was often a struggle. Not only did we have to eat liver, but we had to live in an old house with so little insulation that we could feel the wind blow through the walls in the winter. The house had a space heater, but the space it sat in seemed to be the only space it heated. We slept under six inches of quilts and blankets.

Surely life would improve if only we had more money.

CAN MONEY BUY HAPPINESS?

Although many of us may believe more money always means more happiness, some studies disagree. Research has shown that after basic needs are met—food, shelter, health care—more money doesn't necessarily mean more happiness. In fact, it indicates that the more money you have, the less successful it is in producing joy. Going from an income of $20,000 a year to $50,000 may double your happiness quotient, but then increasing it to $90,000 generates only a blip on the happiness scale.[1] We need money to buy the essentials of life, but once those are met, the best things in life really are free or inexpensive: holding your spouse's hand on a nightly walk, coffee and conversation with a friend, viewing a breathtaking sunset.

Just a Little More

Probably most of us think life would be easier if only we had a little more money. With a bigger savings account, we could sleep better at night. We could get ahead of the bills, ahead of our debt, ahead of our neighbors.

Many studies have been done on how much money it takes to make someone feel wealthy, and the results have been surprisingly consistent. Almost everyone feels they would have enough if they had just twice what they have now.[2] The worker making $25,000 would think himself rich if he made $50,000. The person with $2 million in the bank would feel he had enough if he had $4 million.

While most of us wish we had more money, we might not see ourselves as having a problem with handling our personal funds. Not many of us would admit to having an issue with greed. One reason for this is that our culture requires us to use money. We need money to pay for the necessities of food, clothes, and shelter. Money to go to school, money to get to work. Therefore, we rationalize we need *more* money. We simply don't have enough.

But also, we may not see our problem with money because we spend most of our time with people in our same socioeconomic bracket. We live in the same neighborhoods, shop in the same stores, attend the same churches. We tend to measure ourselves against the friend who came to lunch with a designer-label purse on her arm or the neighbor who parks a new SUV in his driveway instead of comparing ourselves with the single mom struggling to feed her kids with food stamps or the retiree on a fixed income who is trying to make ends meet.

My daughter and her family live in China. To see them, we have taken several trips to the other side of the world. On one of our trips, we went on an excursion to see Dadieshui—a beautiful waterfall I had learned about on the internet. Simply getting to Dadieshui was an adventure. The driver we hired didn't know exactly how to get there, so he drove in the general direction of the waterfall. At every crossroads, he stopped, leaned out of the window, and asked a pedestrian, "Dadieshui?" After we bounced over many miles of potholes, the road simply stopped. We saw a sign that read "Dadieshui," so we knew we were at the right place. But workers were rebuilding the road to the waterfall (laying paving tiles by hand!), so we needed to walk the rest of the way. At first, we walked along the side of the road-in-progress, but eventually even that devolved into an unpaved path that went past a little hut. The owner of the hut sat in front of his home, cooking his dinner over an open fire. The path to Dadieshui essentially went directly through this man's kitchen.

> Money is not evil in and of itself, but our pursuit of it, our attachment to it, can get in the way of our relationship with God. Money can become an idol—something we worship instead of the one true God.

When I watch my favorite home makeover shows on HGTV, I drool over the grand cupboards and lavish counter space of gourmet kitchens. But that day when I compared my kitchen with this Chinese kitchen, I realized God's generous blessings to me. Much of my problem with "enough" in the area of money comes from comparing myself with the wrong group of people.

Money can be a monster issue in our lives. Jesus knew that. In fact, He preached on money often, saying "You cannot serve God and money" (Matthew 6:24). Money wasn't a big deal to Him, but He knew it would be to us.

Not only can the love of money injure our relationship with God, but it may also shatter human relationships. Money often sparks tension in marriages. In his book *Money, Possessions, and Eternity*, author Randy Alcorn reports that 80 percent of divorced people claim financial problems as a major contributor in ending their marriages.[3]

Thankfully, because my husband and I are both famously frugal, money rarely triggers conflict. In fact, when I first sat down to write this chapter,

I thought it would be a snap because I believed enough money was not my struggle. Other "enoughs" loom larger in my battle with contentment. But the more I dug into the story of the rich fool, the more I saw myself in the tale. As I studied Jesus' words, I recalled times when I did wrestle with the issue of money. I remembered my wish for more cash as newlyweds. My anxiety over house payments when we moved from Montana to Illinois without being able to sell our Montana home. My worries over paying college tuition for our children. My "less than" feelings when friends and family found high-paying jobs and I was "just" a piano teacher. Like the rich fool, I have looked to money for answers found only in the God of sufficiency.

This is the most common idol on earth. He who has money and possessions feels secure . . . and is joyful and undismayed as though he were sitting in the midst of Paradise. On the other hand, he who has no money doubts and is despondent, as though he knew of no God. —Martin Luther[4]

Money in the Bible

In the English Standard Version of the Bible, there are 129 verses about money, 433 verses that mention gold, 283 verses that talk about silver, and 169 verses containing the word *rich* for a total of 1,014 verses about wealth.

Why do you think the Bible talks so much about wealth?

_____

_____

_____

_____

_____

_____

The Idol of Money

Jesus told the parable of the rich fool in response to a man who came to the Teacher with a request for a judgment between him and his brother.

> Someone in the crowd said to Him, "Teacher, tell my brother to divide the inheritance with me." But He said to him, "Man, who made Me a judge or arbitrator over you?" And He said to them, "Take care, and be on your guard against all covetousness, for one's life does not consist in the abundance of his possessions." (Luke 12:13–15)

In any case, Jesus declined to judge on worldly wealth. He cared more about the man's soul than his bank account, and He took the opportunity to teach the man and the rest of the crowd about true wealth. He told them to "guard against all covetousness." The Greek word for "covetousness," *pleonexia,* can also be translated as "greed." It's the desire to have more and more and still more. It's the absence of enough.

Jesus saw the man's heart and saw greed. The man wanted more money. Money in itself is not corrupt. Rich people are not inherently evil. Wealthy God-followers like Abraham, David, and the women who supported Jesus' ministry appear in the pages of the Bible.

Pleonexia is the desire to have more and more and still more. It's the absence of enough.

The problem comes when money is no longer simply a tool but an object of desire. The apostle Paul wrote to his protégé Timothy, "The love of money is a root of all kinds of evils" (1 Timothy 6:10). Money becomes an idol when our greed—our quest for more—leads us to worship and trust money more than God.

Perhaps you do not consider money a personal problem. Like I did, you may think, *Money is not one of my idols.* But answer this question: Do you feel you have enough money? Ecclesiastes 5:10 says:

> He who loves money will not be satisfied with money, nor
> he who loves wealth with his income; this also is vanity.

I think many of us would admit to wanting more. Like the people in the study I mentioned before, we might feel wealthy if only we had twice as much as we have now.

Exercising Enough

How would you answer these three questions?

Do I have money in the bank but no peace in my soul?

_____

Do I often think, *If I had X amount of money, I would be satisfied?*

_____

Do I have a difficult time giving money away?[5]

_____

Explain your answers.

_____

_____

_____

_____

And if I admit I occasionally worship at the altar of wealth, I find it helpful to ask one more question: *Why* has money become an idol? Or *why* has money become so important in my life?

As a newlywed, I would have answered, "So I don't have to eat liver every week." But even after my husband and I finished school and began earning enough to eliminate that meal from our menus, I admit sometimes I was not satisfied with our income.

For me, this dissatisfaction stemmed from a desire for security. When the statement from the bank announced a larger total in our checking account, I felt safer. A greater amount in the bank meant a greater ability to take care of ourselves. With more money, I felt more in control of my life. (That was very important to this admitted control freak.)

For others, more money may mean greater status. Greater wealth gives the ability to afford the car that gets noticed at valet parking or the bling that friends drool over at lunch. Personal affluence can open doors to private clubs and the opportunity to socialize with the elite. It can give the ability to subtly drop comments about going to the ritzy health spa, taking the Caribbean cruise, and scoring the impossible-to-get-tickets for a popular musical.

Examining why money sometimes becomes an object of worship in our lives can uncover deep-rooted idols in our lives—idols of security or status. Once we have identified these false gods, we can then go to the true God of sufficiency to topple them over.

I felt safer with more money in the bank. Even now I tend to act as if paying the bills and putting food on the table were all up to me and my husband. I'm inclined to ignore the fact that God generously gives me all my blessings. Jesus told His followers, "Do not seek what you are to eat and what you are to drink, nor be worried. For all the nations of the world seek after these things, and your Father knows that you need them" (Luke 12:29–30). God desires that we view Him as the giver of all good gifts and the supplier of all our needs. He wants to free us from the prison of wanting more and more. He longs for us to experience the freedom of living a life of trust.

True significance doesn't come from owning expensive things or being able to afford the best. There's nothing wrong with buying a nice car or sparkling gem, but we don't need to find our status in the size of our bank account. Our significance comes from realizing that as children of God's family, we are royalty—sons and daughters of the Most High King. The apostle Paul tells us in Galatians, "In Christ Jesus you are all sons of God, through faith" (Galatians 3:26), and that as His sons and daughters, we are heirs in the heavenly kingdom (Galatians 4:7).

Prayer Prompt

First, examine the role money plays in your life. Why does it sometimes assume the role of idol? Are you more likely to view it as a source of security? a means to obtain status? the power to buy more things?

_____

_____

Now, write a prayer asking the Holy Spirit to help you push away the idol of money and to find security, status, and satisfaction in the loving Father.

_____

_____

_____

The Transience of Money

In the parable Jesus told, the rich man clearly trusts in the abundance of his grain and goods as the source of his security and enjoyment. He tells himself that when he has "ample goods laid up for many years," *then* he can be happy (Luke 12:19). Wealth acted as his security blanket.

But God reminds the rich man of the transience of wealth: "Fool! This night your soul is required of you, and the things you have prepared, whose will they be?" (v. 20).

While on earth, we work and toil for money, but in the end, we can't take it with us. Dollars, euros, and yuan are not heavenly currencies.

In my piano studio, students come weekly to make music. Learning to play an instrument is fun, but it is also a long process requiring years of practice. To keep students motivated, I reward them with "piano dollars" when they complete practice goals. I print this special currency on green paper, and the students use the dollars to buy prizes in my little "store."

> God wants to free us from the prison of wanting more and more. He longs for us to experience the freedom of living a life of trust.

Most of my students spend their dollars right away on candy or little trinkets I find at the party store. Some of them save the dollars for a few weeks so they can buy a bigger prize, like a stuffed animal or piece of jewelry. But what if a student continued to save and save his piano dollars so he could eventually go to Best Buy and purchase a new gaming console or cool new phone?

He would be foolish. Much as I wish they would, my photocopied piano dollars won't work at Best Buy.

How often we act like that hypothetical student. We work for more and more money, stockpiling it for the future, even though we can't take it with us when we die. It has no value in heaven.

Not only is money not eternal, but it can be easily lost here on earth. Thieves and scams may steal our money. Bad economies may devalue it. Even though we accumulate money, we have no guarantee of its value.

Jesus called the rich man in the parable a fool because he had not prepared for eternity. He had based his security on what he could pile up on earth. He spent all of his time on the temporary things of life without giving a thought to the eternal.

Jesus asks us to have an eternal perspective. Our heavenly Father wants us to understand that what our eyes can now perceive is actually not real. He longs to give us eyes to view what is truly lasting. God reminds us this life is just a blip of time compared to eternity.

═══ WEALTH IN BIBLE TIMES ═══

In Bible times, wealth was most often tied to property holdings. The poor had just enough land to live on and to grow the bare minimum of food. In contrast, the wealthy had vast property holdings, which they either inherited or received through payment of debts. This land could be leased out for extra income or used to grow surplus food that could be sold for a profit.

In New Testament times, wealth was often seen as a sign of God's blessing. Therefore, the wealthy were viewed as righteous. But Jesus' words often contradicted that belief, as when He said, "It is easier for a camel to go through the eye of a needle than for a rich person to enter the kingdom of God" (Mark 10:25).

Wealth can be a blessing, but it can also be a hindrance to God's kingdom.

Rich toward God

Jesus understood the fleeting value of money, so He encouraged His listeners to be rich in a different way. At the end of the story—after God informs the hoarder of wealth of his foolishness because his life is now required of him—Jesus says, "So is the one who lays up treasure for himself and is not rich toward God" (Luke 12:21). Through the parable, Jesus informs us of the foolishness of stockpiling something as transient as money. Our earthly wealth will do us no good in heaven and may even be counterproductive if it interferes with our relationship with the eternal Lord of heaven and earth.

Instead, Jesus encourages us to be rich toward God. What does that mean? What does it look like to be rich toward God? In Greek, the word translated "toward" is *eis*, which can also mean "in." In his commentary on Luke, R. C. H. Lenski writes:

> To be rich in God is to have the wealth that is found in God. This
> wealth consists of pardon, peace, and salvation in union with God,

and "in God" signifies faith. That individual is rich in God who has the saving gifts which God gives him and holds them with gratitude by faith as his own. Such a man is truly rich, however little he may have of earthly goods.[6]

When I realize how the God of sufficiency has already provided enough for me in eternity, I am rich in God. The Father spent the life of His own Son so I could possess salvation. Jesus paid the ultimate price so I could have eternal joy.

Knowing and appreciating the truth that I am eternally rich *in* God—rich in the things that truly matter—can lead me to a life that is rich *toward* God. I begin to use my earthly wealth in God-honoring ways. When I generously share, holding money with an open hand instead of a closed fist, I am rich toward God.

> While on earth, we work and toil for money, but in the end, we can't take it with us.

When the rich man in Jesus' parable received an abundant harvest, his first thought could have been, *Now that I have more than enough for myself, I can give some away to others in need.* Instead he chose to build bigger barns and hoard it for himself.

The Bible does advise us to save for the future. Proverbs 13:11 tells us, "Wealth gained hastily will dwindle, but whoever gathers little by little will increase it," and Proverbs 6:6–8 says, "Go to the ant, O sluggard; consider her ways, and be wise. Without having any chief, officer, or ruler, she prepares her bread in summer and gathers her food in harvest." The wise save up in times of plenty for the times of scarcity.

But we need to find a balance between saving and hoarding. Saving enough for retirement, saving enough for the proverbial rainy day, is wise. But when does saving become hoarding? Perhaps when we save "enough," we think we can get along without God. We may feel so secure in our own resources that we don't sense an overwhelming reliance on the One who owns it all.

Storing money can lead to danger, for the more money we pile up, the more it grabs our hearts. We can loosen money's grip by giving it away—by viewing our material goods in terms of how they might help those in need. Recently, one of my small-group Bible study members told us about seeing a picture of a celebrity carrying a $45,000 gym bag. Thousands of dollars spent on something to hold smelly gym socks! As a group, we speculated how the money could be better spent. One woman surmised that amount of money would probably feed an African village for a year.

GIVING IN THE BIBLE

In the Old Testament, under the Law of Moses, Israelites were required to offer a tenth of their harvest and a tenth of their flocks and herds to the Lord (Leviticus 27:30–34). They also gave additional offerings to atone for their sins and to offer thanks (Leviticus 4, 6).

In the New Testament, Jesus praised the widow who put two very small copper coins into the temple treasury because she gave all she had (Luke 21:1–4). Many first-century Christians sold everything they had and gave to anyone in need (Acts 2:45).

We worship the Provider by giving back some of what we have received from Him. But whatever we give, we should give from the heart. In 2 Corinthians 9:7, we read, "Each one must give as he has decided in his heart, not reluctantly or under compulsion, for God loves a cheerful giver."

We might not purchase thousand-dollar gym bags, but we can consider how the money we spend might be better used. Eight dollars can buy a sandwich at a café or one day at a safe house for a woman rescued from human trafficking. Fifty dollars provides dinner for two at a nice restaurant or feeds a family for two weeks at a local food pantry.[7] Seventy dollars will buy the new pair of boots I saw online or provide food, clean water, health care, and education for a child in a developing country for two months.

In Jesus' teaching after the parable of the rich fool, He said:

> Sell your possessions, and give to the needy. Provide yourselves with moneybags that do not grow old, with a treasure in the heavens that does not fail, where no thief approaches and no moth destroys. For where your treasure is, there will your heart be also. (Luke 12:33–34)

He didn't say, "Sell *all* your possessions." At another time, Jesus did give this instruction to a rich young ruler because that man's wealth prevented him from following God (Mark 10:21), but most of us need to find a balance between giving everything away and being like the rich fool who kept everything for himself. Proverbs 30:8–9 has a helpful prayer for us:

Remove far from me falsehood and lying; give me neither poverty nor riches; feed me with the food that is needful for me, lest I be full and deny You and say, "Who is the LORD?" or lest I be poor and steal and profane the name of my God.

Giving away our surplus can do two things for us: (1) make us more reliant on God, and (2) tie our hearts to heaven.

We may be tempted to think we don't need God if we have enough money in the bank. We can take care of ourselves, thank you very much. But when we trust in money, we will never have enough. When we rely on it, we will never have true happiness or security.

Instead, Jesus wants us to remember that our Father knows what we need (Luke 12:30) and that He loves to give (v. 32). Satan will continually tempt us to view God as stingy and tightfisted. Daily he will whisper hints of doubt about God's sufficiency in our ears. But as we go to God's Word, we are reminded that He is the God who gives. And as we follow His example of giving, we reaffirm our trust in the God who provides.

> Giving will loosen money's grip on our hearts and tie them to heaven.

Exercising Enough

Learn about disadvantaged people in your community. Pockets of poverty in our cities and suburbs exist where immigrants and refugees may be taken advantage of by landlords. People affected by institutional unfairness and racism may find it hard to make a living wage. We can use our resources to show we care.

But where to start?

Here are some ideas:

♦ Find a community-based organization engaged with vulnerable populations in your city.

♦ Call your county government and tell them you would like to use your passion for children at risk or your skills in financial planning to help the disadvantaged in your area.

♦ Contact the social worker at a local school and offer to take a family without a car to doctor appointments. Be open to inviting an immigrant family to your home for a meal.[8]

Giving will also loosen money's grip on our hearts and tie them to heaven. Jesus said, "Where your treasure is, there your heart will be also" (Matthew 6:21). If we spend our money on a quest for the newest electronic devices and latest fashionable clothes, our hearts will be tied to those. But if we give our resources to help women rescued from brothels in Thailand or issionaries reaching Muslims in Africa, our hearts become knitted to those causes. It is often noted that of the things here on earth, only God's Word and His people are eternal.

Martin Luther said, "I have held many things in my hands, and I have lost them all; but whatever I have placed in God's hands, that I still possess."[9] I often forget this great truth. In God's upside-down kingdom, the path to keeping is giving. The way to true wealth is generosity. Now I ask God to daily remind me that money is only a tool—but a powerful tool that can help those less fortunate and provide the means to spread the Gospel. In the process, money becomes an instrument that gives the God of "enough" all the glory.

Prayer Prompt

Reread Proverbs 30:8–9 and rewrite the prayer in your own words.

The God of Sufficiency

God continually invites me to trust Him as the God of sufficiency. Through His Word, He tells me, "I know life is hard. At every turn, you encounter bills and expenses. You worry about not having enough (Matthew 6:25–28). It's tempting to view money as the answer to all your problems (1 Timothy 6:17). But remember—a love of money can cause unnecessary pain when you work yourself into burnout to obtain more of it, when it threatens to take precedence over important relationships in life, or when it simply lets you down (Ecclesiastes 2:22–23). I promise I will never abandon you. I will never leave you stranded (Hebrews 13:5). I will always supply your needs (Philippians 4:19). I am the Great Provider, the owner of all the cattle on the hillsides and every bird in the sky (Psalm 50:10). All the silver and the gold are Mine (Haggai 2:8). You can live in slavery to money, working constantly in an attempt to get enough (Ecclesiastes 5:10), or you can live in freedom, trusting Me to provide (Matthew 6:31–32)."

> Knowing and appreciating the truth that I am eternally rich *in* God—rich in the things that truly matter—can lead me to a life that is rich *toward* God. I begin to use my earthly wealth in God-honoring ways.

I'm learning to live free. Free from the constant quest for more cash. Free from seeking security in the total in my savings account. (Also free from weekly meals of liver, thank You, God!)

And I'm learning to live rich. Rich in God's grace and salvation. Rich in the knowledge that the Owner of everything sees me and knows my needs. Rich in being a baptized daughter of the King.

May you, too, live rich and free.

WHAT IS YOUR BIGGEST TAKEAWAY FROM THIS CHAPTER?

O GOD OF SUFFICIENCY,

You are the Great Provider, owning the cattle on a thousand hills and everything else I might need. I praise You for You have already made me rich in Christ, as an heir to Your glorious kingdom.

I confess I have often based my security and status on the total in my bank account or on owning expensive things. Instead of living in trust of Your provision, I have viewed money as the solution to my problems. I have allowed the accumulation of money to take precedence over my relationship with You and Your people.

Thank You, Lord, for teaching me to live free of this burden for more and more. Help me to continually trust Your goodness and generosity and Your miraculous ability to provide. In Jesus' name. Amen.

CHAPTER 3

ENOUGH STUFF

Memory Verse:
And He said to them, "Take care, and be on your guard against all covetousness, for one's life does not consist in the abundance of his possessions." Luke 12:15

"O say can you see . . ." The toy in the backseat sang out the national anthem for the 101st time. We felt we would go crazy if we heard it 102 times.

It was Christmastime—that joyous season of consumerism. Three days before the nonstop recital of "The Star-Spangled Banner," my husband and I had packed up our four-year-old daughter and almost-two-year-old son in our little fire-engine-red Nissan Sentra to drive from our home in Illinois to see grandparents in Wisconsin.

Grandparents love to spoil their grandchildren, and how could I limit their joy? But that year the abundance of gifts became overwhelming. It was the year my younger sister worked at a toy factory (as a receptionist, not an elf). Right before the holidays, the factory announced it needed to close due to the bad economy. My sister would soon lose her job, but not before she had the opportunity to buy some of the company's wares. To sell off their inventory, the factory offered deep discounts to employees and their families. My parents accompanied my sister to the closing sale and, I'm pretty sure, bought one of every toy available. (I come from a long line of people who simply cannot resist a good deal.)

The factory specialized in classic, quality wooden toys, so that year my children received wooden blocks, dominoes, train sets, and puzzles. One puzzle contained all fifty US states and played the national anthem when the puzzle was completed. *How cute*, we thought when our daughter opened the gift.

But when the time came to go home, not all the toys would fit in the small Sentra trunk. So, we stacked the extras in the backseat between the car seats with the United States puzzle on the top of the pile. However, we didn't realize the chip that played "The Star-Spangled Banner" was light-sensitive and the puzzle piece that covered the chip had moved off in the shuffle of packing. Every time a semi passed us, its lights cued up the anthem. I couldn't reach the puzzle from the front seat, and the kids had fallen asleep, so we didn't want to stop. As much as we love our national anthem, we quickly grew tired of it. If a convoy of trucks zoomed by, the song would start over with each pair of headlights. "O say can you . . . O say can . . . O say . . ." It was the purgatory of patriotism.

While I vividly remember that United States puzzle, I also recall the sheer number of toys our children received that Christmas. When we finally got home, it took us days to find places to store them because, truthfully, the toy box was already full. We appreciated my parents' generosity, and our kids loved all the new playthings, but it became the beginning of too much stuff.

WHAT ENERGIZES YOU MOST—COLLECTING THINGS OR GETTING RID OF THINGS? WHY?

Not only did our children have too many toys to fit in the toy box, but I had too many dishes for my limited cupboards and too many clothes for my tiny closet.

Yet, I bought more. Because I discovered thrift stores.

Like my parents, I cannot resist a good deal. When I went to the local resale shop, I could easily come home with twenty new-to-me items. Twenty fashionable items. Twenty thrifty items. Twenty items I didn't need.

Maybe you can relate. We all have stuff. We buy stuff. We store stuff. We may even feel overwhelmed by the amount of stuff.

Part of the problem comes with wanting more. We are like my niece when she was about two years old. She loved Saturday-morning cartoons, and whenever a commercial for a cool new plaything interrupted the cartoon, she screamed with the intensity of a battery-operated toy fire engine, "I want it! I NEED it!" We've all behaved like that at one time or another. We see a beautiful sweater, an amazing tool, or—my personal weakness—a stunning pair of shoes, and suddenly our satisfaction dies like a AA battery on Christmas morning. We NEED that new item.

To compound the problem, we may also find it difficult to get rid of possessions we no longer need or use. We see the apple corer in the drawer. Yes, we haven't used the gadget in fifteen years. *But who knows?* we reason. *Next year someone might ask us to bake a hundred apple pies, and wouldn't that corer come in handy?*

> We buy stuff.
> We store stuff.
> We may even feel overwhelmed by the amount of stuff.

Because of my penchant for thrift shops, I have now become fairly efficient at tossing unused belongings in order to make room for my new purchases. But I live with someone who is purge-challenged. When my husband and I tune in to watch an episode of *Hoarders,* he laughingly calls it his favorite how-to show. It may be a joke, but I have stopped donating our castoffs to our church rummage sale. It wasn't a very effective way of getting rid of things because, as pastor of the church, my husband would have an early peek at the merchandise and invariably would come home holding one of the things I had donated, saying, "Look what I just bought at the rummage sale. We used to have one just like it!"

Many of us have an addiction to stuff. We want to buy it. We like to own it. We need to store it. Why do we feel this need for things? Part of this desire certainly stems from living in a materialistic society. Advertisements tell us that we deserve a better watch. That our loved ones will appreciate us only if they receive a diamond necklace. That our significance is entirely dependent on the type of car we drive.

Satan knows the more he keeps us busy buying, cleaning, organizing, dusting, filing, washing, arranging, displaying, polishing, tuning, vacuuming, repairing, painting, and maintaining our possessions, the less time we may have for our relationship with God.

With these messages constantly bombarding us, we start to believe—at least a little bit—that our lives will not matter until we own the next status symbol. Satan keeps us in the stores and online with the lie that the more we own, the more happiness we'll possess. He does this because he knows our quest for things will distract us from what is truly important. Benjamin Franklin wrote, "The more a man has, the more he wants. Instead of filling a vacuum, it makes one."[1] Satan knows the more he keeps us busy buying, cleaning, organizing, dusting, filing, washing, arranging, displaying, polishing, tuning, vacuuming, repairing, painting, and maintaining our possessions, the less time we may have for our relationship with God.

Unfortunately, even when our drawers, closets, garages, and storage units are full, we may discover we still don't have what we've been looking for. We still don't have enough.

The main character in Jesus' parable in Luke 12 had a problem with enough stuff. And like many of us, he didn't see the problem. Not unlike a modern-day hoarder who rents space in a storage facility to save more stuff, the rich fool built bigger barns to store his grain and his goods. He felt he needed the additional possessions to guarantee an enjoyable life. And surely the bigger barns became tangible proof of his prosperity.

Jesus told this story because He knew the people in His day and the people in our day would have difficulty as spiritual beings living in a material world. What can we learn about our stuff from this rich fool?

The Problem of Possessions

When the rich man experienced an overabundant harvest, he responded, "What shall I do, for I have nowhere to store my crops? . . . I will do this: I will tear down my barns and build larger ones, and there I will store all my grain and my goods" (Luke 12:17–18). What little word do you see repeated? *My. My* crops. *My* barns. *My* grain. *My* goods.

He viewed all the blessings he had received as belonging to him to do with as he pleased.

We all like to possess things. A well-established phenomenon in psychology known as the "endowment effect" demonstrates that we value an object much more if we own it. In one study, students were given a chocolate bar or a coffee mug as a reward for helping with research. When given the choice, half chose the mug and half the chocolate. The two rewards seemed to be of equal value. But when students were given the mug first and later had the opportunity to exchange for the chocolate (or the other way around), the majority opted to keep what they had. Even though the rewards seemed to be of equal value, nearly all the participants chose to hang on to what they started out with.[2] We don't want to give up what we own. We want what is *ours*.

What does the Bible say about ownership? Psalm 24:1 tells us:

> The earth is the LORD's and the fullness thereof, the world,
> and those who dwell therein.

<hr>

BARNS IN BIBLE TIMES

The word translated "barn" in Luke 12 is *apothéké*. This term describes any place used to store grain and may also be translated as "storehouse," "granary," or "garner." In Bible times, these places were sometimes below ground, sometimes above. At the archaeological site of Gezer in Palestine, excavators found circular aboveground granaries in a variety of sizes.[3]

<hr>

We tend to think of things in terms of *my* house, *my* clothes, *my* car. After all, we worked hard to obtain those possessions. We put in thousands of hours at the computer, at the cash register, at the café to earn our things.

But we often forget God gave us not only the opportunity for the job we have but the talent and ability to perform the work. All the things we have and enjoy are gifts from our heavenly Father (Deuteronomy 8:18).

What would happen if we accepted the truth that God is the true owner of everything and we are only stewards of what God has given us? Would we have less of a compulsion to obtain more and more? Would we share more and hoard less? Would we let go of the sense of entitlement? Could we hold the things of this world more loosely? Would we feel a responsibility to use the assets He has placed in our hands to help those who have less?

Later in Luke 12, after the parable of the rich fool, Jesus talks about a faithful servant who is given the job of taking care of the household while the master is away. The master expects the servant to manage the household assets faithfully. Each one of us is that servant. God asks us to use *His* goods—the possessions He gives to us—to care for His people. Jesus adds, "Everyone to whom much was given, of him much will be required, and from him to whom they entrusted much, they will demand the more" (Luke 12:48). Blessings come with responsibility. What has God entrusted you with? What is He asking of you?

Prayer Prompt

Write a prayer asking God to help you make wise use of the things He has entrusted to you.

_____

_____

_____

_____

_____

_____

_____

_____

More Doesn't Equal Happiness

After the rich fool made his plan to build bigger barns to store more goods, he told himself, "You have ample goods laid up for many years; relax, eat, drink, be merry" (Luke 12:19). In other words, his motto was "When I have enough stuff stored up, *then* I will have happiness."

He sounds like so many of us in this modern age of acquisition. We might not say it aloud, but we tell ourselves, "When my kitchen looks like the one in *Architectural Digest*, then I'll be satisfied," or "If I could afford those designer jeans, then I would be happy," or "When we can finally take that dream Hawaiian vacation, then I'll know we've made it." We feel we must attain a certain amount of money, possessions, or status before we can truly enjoy life.

> The truth is, we are rarely satisfied even when we get the very thing we've been dreaming about.

But more does not always equal happiness. The truth is, we are rarely satisfied even when we get the very thing we've been dreaming about. We simply move on to the next thing on our wish list. This is nothing new. Even in the 1800s, the famous preacher Charles Spurgeon said, "You say, 'If I had a little more, I should be very satisfied.' You make a mistake. If you are not content with what you have, you would not be satisfied if it were doubled."[4]

Some people are recognizing this fact and are making a U-turn from our society's quest for more by embracing minimalism. Maybe you've watched a few episodes of *Tiny House* and marveled at how people can live without walk-in closets or kitchen cupboards. Perhaps you've read about the one-hundred-thing challenge where those who take the dare own a total of one hundred things. I don't think I could do it. I just went into my closet and counted forty-seven T-shirts!

These minimalists may be taking things to an extreme, but they realize that *more* doesn't necessarily mean happiness. In his book *Simplify*, minimalist blogger Joshua Becker tells a story about taking groups of people on short-term mission trips. He writes that invariably he will hear people expressing their feelings with comments like these:

"How can people who have so little be so joyful?"

"I wish I could enjoy life as much as they do!"

"I'm so blessed to live in America where I'm able to have so many more possessions."

Joshua Becker says few will realize the ironic connection in their comments and will understand that more possessions do not automatically mean more happiness.[5] Perhaps we can find more joy in less.

Exercising Enough

Many of us will admit to having too many things. One way to help us curb our pursuit of more is to set limits. Knowing my penchant for shoes, my husband has jokingly limited me to twenty-five pairs. While he doesn't enforce the limit, I find it useful. It makes me get rid of some old shoes when I find a new pair. (And I'm always tempted to find a new pair!) Try setting limits in items you tend to collect. This will prevent your closets and cupboards from overflowing!

Take a minute to contemplate:

Items I tend to collect:

_____

_____

_____

Limits I will set:

_____

_____

Jonah 2:8 says, "Those who pay regard to vain idols forsake their hope of steadfast love." Our stuff can become idols—things we worship, things we go to for joy, things we believe we can't live without. But when we turn toward those worthless idols, we turn away from God's love. In effect, we are saying to God, "This house, this car, this designer handbag is more crucial to my happiness than You." God's love is always there, waiting for us, but we forsake it.

> Gratitude is what makes whatever we have enough.

However, Jonah doesn't leave us there. He goes on: "But I with the voice of thanksgiving will sacrifice to You" (Jonah 2:9). Thanksgiving is what makes those worthless idols fade in importance. Gratitude is what makes whatever we have enough.

Lately I've been trying to thank God for each item I possess. As I get ready in the morning, I thank God for my hair dryer that helps me get ready more quickly. As I cook dinner, I say a prayer of gratitude for my ordinary peeler that makes quick work of preparing carrots. This simple practice doesn't take much time, but each word of thankfulness reminds me how rich I truly am *now*.

Gratitude for what I have makes me realize I don't have to postpone my happiness until I have more. I can take joy in what I have. It is enough.

The Soul Is Not Made for Things

In Jesus' parable, when the rich fool says, "You have ample goods laid up for many years; relax, eat, drink, be merry" (Luke 12:19), he is addressing his soul. He, like many of us, misunderstood the nature of the soul.

In Greek, the word translated "soul" is *psyche*—it is the part of us that is eternal and the seat of our feelings and desires. Matthew Henry writes in his commentary of Luke 12, "The things of the world will not suit the nature of a soul, nor supply its needs, nor satisfy its desires, nor last so long as it will last."[6] We cannot satisfy our souls with more possessions.

In fact, more things may actually weigh down our souls and our minds. Psychologists have found that unchecked clutter in our homes can lead to depression and anxiety.[7] UCLA researchers discovered stress hormones spiked in the brains of mothers when they dealt with their belongings.[8] Those stress chemicals (which often result from disorganization) eat up the beneficial chemicals in our brains that stabilize our emotions.[9] Every single thing we own can add a heaviness to our tired souls.

Most of us realize this burden of excess on our minds and souls. And yet we have trouble getting rid of our stuff. What to keep? What to discard? A very popular book titled *The Life-Changing Magic of Tidying Up* (not a book I recommend, by the way) suggests holding up each item you own and asking yourself, "Does it spark joy?" This can be a useful question. Yes, my favorite gray cardigan sparks joy. It fits me well. It keeps me warm. It coordinates with many of my other clothes. On the other hand, the red satin top I bought to go with one of my blazers does not spark joy. It's beautiful but didn't actually work with the intended blazer and doesn't look good with anything else

I own. I should get rid of it, but I paid a lot of money for it and I feel I should wear it at least once. That item only sparks regret.

"Does it spark joy?" can be a practical assessment, but minimalist blogger Becker suggests a better question would be "Does it help me fulfill a greater purpose in life?"[10] This question asks how our possessions can help or hinder our life goals, rather than simply focusing on personal happiness.

But I would like to suggest that even better questions would be these: How does this item affect my soul? Does it draw me closer to the God of sufficiency, or does it pull me away? These questions will require some careful thought. For instance, a classic car could be seen as something that pulls the owner away from God. It requires large sums of money and weekends filled with maintenance tasks. Working on the car could isolate the owner from his family and keep him from attending Sunday services. On the other hand, a pair of hiking boots could be seen as an item that draws the owner closer to God. When she wears the boots, she is experiencing nature and witnessing God's glorious creation. Her heart fills with praise for the Lord of the universe.

But the opposite could be true as well. Perhaps the classic car owner uses the hours spent maintaining his vehicle as quality time with his son or daughter in their shared interest. Maybe he takes this prized possession to classic car shows designed to spark conversations about Jesus to the unchurched. And the owner of the hiking boots? Maybe she's the one missing church every weekend to spend time in the great outdoors.

When you begin decluttering or before you purchase something new, determine how each item draws you closer to God or pulls you farther away. Does the item weigh down your soul as one more thing to dust and clean? Or does it fill your heart with gratitude each time you see it? Does it pull you away from time with your heavenly Father? Or does it make life easier, giving you more time with the Savior? Is it a useful tool, saving you time or money that can be used for the Kingdom?

In Luke 14, Jesus told a parable about a man who prepared a great banquet and invited many guests. However, when the time for the banquet arrived, the guests all sent their regrets. One had bought a field. Another had purchased a yoke of oxen. Going to see these purchases took precedence over attending the banquet. The parable invites us to look at our lives closely: Is our stuff more important than our relationship with God?

DISSATISFACTION AND DESIRE

Our culture encourages the accumulation of things. "Peer pressure and even advertising often encourage us to be dissatisfied with what we have. We crave other things in order to keep up appearances or to look for happiness and satisfaction in something new."[11] It is not wrong to want and desire. Luther says, "God encourages us to seek His blessings of food, shelter, good jobs, health, success, and so on for ourselves and our family."[12] But we need to remember "that covetousness, or evil desire, is a form of idolatry."[13]

Exercising Enough

To assess how your stuff may be weighing down your soul, pack some of it away for a while. Put some of your books or dishes or home decor in a box in the basement for a week or two. Pay attention to your feelings. Do you miss those items? Or does your soul feel lighter without the clutter?

The God of Sufficiency

We've all seen the bumper sticker that reads, "The one who dies with the most toys wins." Many people live as though this were true, accumulating cars, boats, clothes, shoes, computers, and high-tech devices. But those of us who trust in Christ know earthly possessions are only temporary. In the Luke 12 parable, God told the rich man, "Fool! This night your soul is required of you, and the things you have prepared, whose will they be?" (v. 20). We can't take all the toys and tech gadgets with us. The clothes and computers won't guarantee our happiness.

I have a long way to go in this area. I routinely clean out my closets, cupboards, and basement. But I still have an abundance of things—many, many more than a hundred items! In my heart, there is a battle because I know my soul would feel lighter if I owned less, but part of me often wants more.

I still have a broken wanter. And that wanter will continue to whisper that the acquisition of the next beautiful thing will fill my empty heart, the next desirable item will heal my loneliness. Deep inside I know nothing I own can stock the barren cupboards of my soul, and yet, I succumb again and again to the devil's lies and my own disordered desires.

It's then that I need to remind myself of Jesus' words: "One's life does not consist in the abundance of his possessions" (Luke 12:15). Even though the world tries to define me by the bag I carry or the house I live in, God tells me the truth. I am defined by my position as a child of God, and all my true riches are stored in heaven.

Prayer Prompt

Write a prayer asking God to help you see how your possessions draw you closer to Him or pull you away.

_____

_____

_____

_____

_____

If I rest in this knowledge, I can be content. Instead of a temporary high from scoring the next item on my wish list, I can possess joy and peace as eternal gifts from the Father. The apostle Paul wrote in his Letter to the Philippians, "I have learned in whatever situation I am to be content" (Philippians 4:11). He found this contentment "in any and every circumstance," whether he was "facing plenty [or] hunger, abundance [or] need" (v. 12). How could he do this? By going to God for the power to be satisfied with what he had: "I can do all things through Him who strengthens me" (v. 13). Even when your bathroom has thirty-year-old chipped tile, even when your car has more rust than paint, even when the pantry has nothing but a box of macaroni and cheese, you can learn contentment when you lean on the God of sufficiency.

Jesus reminds us to lean on the Father. He told His followers, "Therefore I tell you, do not be anxious about your life, what you will eat, nor about your body, what you will put on. For life is more than food, and the body more than clothing" (Luke 12:22–23). He reminded them that the Father feeds the ravens and gloriously clothes the flowers of the field and they were much more precious to Him than birds and grass. Jesus urges all of us:

And do not seek what you are to eat and what you are to drink, nor be worried. For all the nations of the world seek after these things, and your Father knows that you need them. Instead, seek His kingdom, and these things will be added to you. (Luke 12:29–31)

I read this and hear Jesus telling me, "You don't have to act like the rest of the world, chasing after things to fill your soul. Rest in the fact that you have a heavenly Father who sees you and knows exactly what you need. Trust Him in this. Don't set your heart on material possessions. Instead, seek out God's kingdom—a kingdom where the size of your house or the price of your car has no relevance. I want you to be rich, but rich in things that matter: peace, joy, love. You can't find these things in a grain elevator or a walk-in closet. They are only found in Me.

"In Me you will find enough."

WHAT IS YOUR BIGGEST TAKEAWAY FROM THIS CHAPTER?

O GOD OF SUFFICIENCY,

Forgive me for when I've looked for my happiness
in the stuff in my closets and cupboards. When I've
regarded all the material blessings You've so graciously
given as mine, mine, mine. When I've allowed things to
become gods and let them pull me away from You, the
one true God.

Thank You for the material gifts You have bestowed.
Help me to live in thanksgiving for what You have
already given and not in constant search for more.
Send Your Spirit to remind me that You know exactly
what I need. Help me to live in trust of Your goodness.

The world may define me by the size of my house
or the price of my jewelry, but Your Word constantly
reminds me of my worth in Christ. May I always find
my "enough" in You. In Jesus' name. Amen.

CHAPTER 4

ENOUGH FOOD

Memory Verse:
And do not seek what you are to eat and what you are to drink, nor be worried. . . . Instead, seek His kingdom, and these things will be added to you.

Luke 12:29, 31

My father had an expression that always made us laugh no matter how many times we heard it. After a holiday meal where he had enjoyed a serving of mashed potatoes, three slices of roast beef, a scoop of sweet potatoes, a helping of green beans, four warm crescent rolls, and two slices of apple pie, he would push himself back from the dining room table and declare, "Well, I've spoiled my appetite." Wink.

I'm writing this chapter on food in January—after the holiday season, when I've spoiled my appetite too many times with layered lasagna and sweet cranberry bread and to-die-for chocolate walnut bars. My scale tells me I've indulged my taste buds too often. I have had more than enough food.

You may be experiencing this problem as well. While many people in this world struggle with finding their next meal, if you have the money to buy this book, you are probably not one of them. In the Western world, most of us can afford not only the basics of bread, rice, beans, and milk but also the luxuries of cheesy enchiladas, T-bone steaks, and cookie-dough ice cream.

The temptation of food is real. You might be thinking, *Yeah, when Jesus was in the desert, He resisted Satan's offer of bread, but He wasn't tempted with triple chocolate cheesecake!* Our culture has so many delectable treats that even when we don't have the problem of getting enough food for survival, we still struggle with satisfaction. We can't wait for the next delicious bite. We anticipate the next tantalizing morsel. Enough food? Never.

Food and Spirituality

Perhaps you wonder why I'm even talking about food in a Bible study. After all, food doesn't seem very spiritual, does it? Believe me, I wondered if I should take on this topic—one so many of us wrestle with.

But food plays a big part in Jesus' Luke 12 parable. The rich man in the story built larger barns to store grain. He needed bigger silos to save his abundant crops. He could have given the excess food away, but he feared he wouldn't have enough for himself.

Jesus also addresses the topic of food in His teaching after the parable. He admonishes His followers never to worry about what they will eat. He encourages them to trust the heavenly Father to always provide sufficient nourishment.

As I contemplated the topic of food (not that it is ever far from my thoughts), I was struck by how many times food plays a major role in other Bible stories. Adam and Eve gave up life in Paradise for a piece of forbidden fruit. Joseph stored food in Egypt in preparation for a seven-year famine. Manna from heaven fed the children of Israel every day for forty years. God used ravens as a catering service to feed the prophet Elijah. Jesus changed water into wine and fed five thousand people with a few loaves of bread and some scrawny fish.

In addition, Scripture often uses physical food as a picture of our spiritual needs. In the poetic language of the Psalms, hunger and thirst become metaphors for deeper desires of the spirit. Jesus talked of banquets and feasts to describe the kingdom of heaven.

How sweet are Your words to my taste, sweeter than honey to my mouth! Psalm 119:103

Why all this emphasis on food? Perhaps because we all need food. We all understand the sensations of rumbling stomachs and parched throats. God's Word uses those perceptions of need to teach us. Yes, our stomachs may be complaining and our taste buds craving, but even stronger than those physical desires is our soul's longing for the one true God.

═══ HELP AND RESOURCES ═══

In this chapter, I address garden-variety food issues. If you have an eating disorder or food addiction, this chapter may not be for you. Here are some resources to help you in this area:

- ♦ **FindingBalance.com**
  This site helps people with all kinds of eating disorders, from food addiction to the fear of gaining weight. Digital libraries and online support groups are available here.

- ♦ **NationalEatingDisorders.org**
  Here you can find a help line and screening tool in addition to information about food issues and how to help a loved one with an eating disorder.

- ♦ **EDCatalogue.com**
  This site provides a comprehensive list of articles, organizations, conferences, and books all designed to help those struggling with food issues.

───────────────

Sometimes we get these hungers out of order. My husband and I grew up in very different food environments. While both of our mothers possessed excellent cooking skills, they each had a unique food philosophy. My mother-in-law always reminded us, "Save room for dessert," even while we were passing the potatoes. On the other hand, you can observe my mother's philosophy in the words my five-year-old son used to introduce her to one of his friends: "That's my grandma. She only likes God and vegetables."

My mother's attitude toward eating is that it should reap health benefits. Carrot sticks and broccoli florets certainly nourish our bodies better than dessert—even if the after-dinner treats are carrot cake or apple pie. And God wants us to care for the bodies He has given us.

> Jesus reminded His followers that the key to a full life is not found in abundant amounts of food.

But maybe God's philosophy is more like that of my mother-in-law's. She didn't want us to fill up on the ordinary food. Meat and potatoes were good, but she wanted us to save room for what she thought was best. The lemon chiffon cake she slaved over for an hour. The chocolate candies she spent days creating. The cookies she lovingly prepared and knew we would enjoy.

In the same way, God doesn't want us to spoil our appetites with the ordinary food of the world. Yes, He wants us to enjoy His gifts of healthy and delicious cuisine. He knows we need the nourishment of the food He has provided. But He doesn't want us to become so focused on feeding our bodies and delighting our palates that we forget about our famished souls. The Father doesn't want us to be satisfied with french fries and lasagna. He wants us to yearn for Him. What if our cravings for enough food are meant to draw us to Jesus—the bread of life?

Prayer Prompt

Do you struggle with satisfaction in the area of food? Is it hard for you to get enough? Write a prayer telling God about this problem.

_____

_____

_____

_____

_____

_____

_____

Life Is More Than Food

Too often I stuff myself with the things of this world: money, possessions, food, success. As I gorge on these temporary things, my appetite for the things that matter begins to fade. Too often I reach for the box of cheese crackers when I'm stressed, the package of chocolates when I'm anxious. I feel better for a minute or two. But it doesn't take long before my insides rumble again. Maybe not my stomach, but my soul. Our bodies need food, but our souls need more.

Jesus told the crowd that listened to His parable, "Life is more than food" (Luke 12:23). The rich man in the story was so concerned about having enough food that he expanded his storage system to have plenty for years to come. But Jesus reminded His followers that the key to a full life is not found in abundant amounts of food.

Perhaps the most obvious example of this in Scripture is the account of the Israelites' sojourn in the desert. A month and a half into their journey, Moses and his two million-plus tagalongs ran out of

God had sated their physical hunger but not their appetite.

the food they had brought with them from Egypt. They were hungry, and they let Moses know it.

Moses went to God and He miraculously provided food in the form of bread from heaven that the Israelites called manna. This became their go-to meal for forty years. With the exception of two recorded feasts of quail, it seems manna was the only thing on the menu. Husbands knew it was senseless to ask for their favorite sandwich for lunch. Kids learned there was no use in asking, "What's for dinner?" It seems the only decision for meal preparation was whether to boil or bake the wafers they gathered daily (Exodus 16:23).

In the second year of the journey, some of the "rabble" among the crowd of two million began to crave other food (Numbers 11:4). Even these lower-class people had eaten cucumbers, leeks, fish, melon, onions, and garlic in Egypt (v. 5). And they missed these flavors. They pined for a little variety. God had sated their physical hunger but not their appetite. He had filled their stomachs but had not satisfied their taste buds.

Why? God is God. He could have provided a different food each day. Monday—manna. Tuesday—quail. Wednesday—cucumbers. Thursday—leeks. Friday—double chocolate brownies. But He didn't. Why?

The answer is in Deuteronomy 8:3, where Moses reminds the children of Israel:

> And He humbled you and let you hunger and fed you with manna,
> which you did not know, nor did your fathers know, that He might
> make you know that man does not live by bread alone, but man lives
> by every word that comes from the mouth of the LORD.

I hope it doesn't take forty years of a subsistence diet for me to realize I can't survive on only bread and water or even steak and caviar. My soul's survival depends on a word from God. Yes, my body can exist on bread and cucumbers and meat (and chocolate). But I cannot truly live without God's life-giving words to me. When Jesus quoted this verse in Matthew 4, He used the Greek word *zaō* for the word "live." This word not only means to breathe and not be dead, but to enjoy real life—blessed, endless life with God.[1] Genuine, meaningful life requires the nourishment of God's Holy Word. Sometimes, like the Israelites, I need humbling experiences to recognize that truth.

I can come home from an exhausting day—frustrated with uncooperative students, irritated with long lines at the grocery store, and fed up with traffic—and head to the freezer for the carton of chocolate moose tracks ice cream that is calling my name. Or I can make a beeline to God's Word. Here I can feast on flavors of grace: "My grace is sufficient for you" (2 Corinthians 12:9). I can revel in God's presence: "I will never leave you nor forsake you" (Hebrews 13:5). The Lord can quench my yearnings with His love: "Satisfy us in the morning with Your steadfast love, that we may rejoice and be glad all our days" (Psalm 90:14). He can fill my emptiness with Himself: "God's love has been poured into our hearts through the Holy Spirit who has been given to us" (Romans 5:5). Ice cream might quiet the rumblings of my stomach and the screams of my taste buds, but it won't unravel the stress in my heart or satisfy my soul's craving for peace.

Life is more than food.

Exercising Enough

Read Deuteronomy 8:3. Why did God allow the Israelites to hunger and feed them only with manna?

_____

_____

_____

How could your cravings and yearnings lead you to God?

_____

_____

_____

_____

To Set Your Heart

In Luke 12, Jesus went on to tell the crowd:

Do not seek what you are to eat and what you are to drink, nor be worried. For all the nations of the world seek after these things, and your Father knows that you need them. Instead, seek His kingdom, and these things will be added to you. (Luke 12:29–31)

The word *seek* is from the Greek word *zētēo*, which means "to look for with apprehension, to make every effort to find."[2] Jesus is saying, "Don't focus on food. Don't let yourself become preoccupied with it."

Some of us might be obsessed with raspberry cheesecake or deep-dish pizza. But others might be preoccupied with food in a different way. Just yesterday I read a *Baby Blues* comic where cute little Zoe tells her dad that her friend's family is vegan. She says, "I think we should be vegans too."

Dad tends to some meat on the grill and tells his daughter, "Okay. But you'll have to give up hamburgers and pepperoni pizza." Zoe reconsiders and replies, "In that case, let's just stick with whatever religion we are now."[3]

Healthy eating is important. We want to care for our bodies as temples of the Holy Spirit. And some of us require special diets for specific health conditions. But let's be careful that our vegetarian, vegan, paleo, ketogenic, raw food, or cabbage soup diets do not become our religion—our focus.

═══ FOOD IN BIBLE TIMES ═══

The most basic and essential food of people in Palestine was bread. This staple was usually made with wheat flour, although sometimes the bread was baked with spelt, millet, or barley flour.

Legumes, especially lentils, were an important source of protein. Other vegetables included cucumbers, onions, garlic, leeks, lettuce, and cabbage. Cooks flavored dishes with parsley, dill, mustard, and coriander seed.

Good meat was scarce and not included in everyday meals. Small quantities might be used to flavor soups and stews. Only on special occasions like Passover would a family enjoy roasted meat.

Fresh fish were roasted over an open fire. The Bible doesn't mention chickens, but it is known they were raised in countries bordering Palestine, so it is likely the Israelites also enjoyed poultry and eggs.

People created treats with dough, dried fruits, and honey. They even had sweets similar to our doughnuts—dough fried in olive oil.[4]

And while we're on the topic of food, I want to address the struggles of those suffering from eating disorders. My friend Lee Wolfe Blum writes honestly about her battles in this area in her book *Table in the Darkness*. An innocent attempt to lose the "freshman fifteen" in college ballooned into an obsession with numbers: the number of calories ingested, the number of calories burned with exercise, and the number on the scale. Lee writes,

> We are promised satisfaction only when we crave righteousness.

"By myopically focusing all my energy on my body, I was free from having to deal with any of the real emotional rumblings happening inside—those overwhelming feelings of sadness and lethargy, sprouting from a place I didn't understand and so ignored. The body was my diversion."[5]

Thankfully, Lee found help through counseling, working with a registered dietitian, confiding in good friends, and giving control to God. She discovered strength in surrendering to the Lord and by admitting she was powerless over the eating disorder.

Whether we attempt to quiet the voices in our heads telling us we're not good enough by eating or by not eating, God reaches out to all of us and gently says, "Find your 'enough' in Me. Don't set your hearts on what you eat and drink (or do not eat and drink). Instead, seek Me and My kingdom." In the Sermon on the Mount, Jesus said it this way:

"Blessed are those who hunger and thirst for righteousness, for they shall be satisfied" (Matthew 5:6).

Prayer Prompt

Write a prayer asking God to give you a craving for Him that is stronger than any other desires.

We are promised satisfaction only when we crave righteousness. Righteousness is a right relationship with God—a gift to us through faith in Jesus' death and resurrection. When this life-changing gift becomes my obsession, I can relax in God's presence and love. When my focus is on Jesus' acceptance of me, I no longer need to reach for self-medicating brownies. I no longer evaluate myself by the number on my scale. My satisfaction comes from being saturated with God's love.

Admittedly, I have not always embraced this truth. There have been times in my life when going to the refrigerator seemed easier than going to God. When my husband graduated from seminary, he was assigned to a church in Montana. We were pretty sure that if it wasn't the end of the earth, you could certainly see it from there. Fourteen hundred miles from family and friends, our first few months seemed incredibly lonely and empty. And I tried to fill the emptiness with food.

Of course, it didn't work. Even as my waistline expanded, my heart continued to wither.

Eventually, the warm embrace and welcome of the members of our new church made us feel more at home. But the most effective change came when I learned to take my eyes off what I felt I lacked—friendship—and focus on what I did possess: a relationship with God, a connection that filled my hungry soul. God's promise to always be with me—even in Montana—helped me curb my frequent trips to the refrigerator. Stuffing ourselves with food is often a desperate attempt to quiet the cravings of our hearts, but only the Bread of Life can do that.

Exercising Enough

So, whether you eat or drink, or whatever you do,
do all to the glory of God. (1 Corinthians 10:31)

Practically speaking, how might your life look different if you put this verse into practice? Brainstorm a bit and ask yourself questions like these: What foods would I eat? What would mealtime look like? How would my relationship with food be different?

The God of Sufficiency

Maybe you're thinking, *But I've tried every diet in the book, and I still have a problem controlling my eating.* Sister, I don't want to make you feel guilty about your habits. This is not about counting calories or fitting into smaller clothes. It's about finding satisfaction in the God of "enough" instead of the gods of chocolate layer cake and nachos grande. It's about accepting the fact that our soul cravings cannot be quieted by money, sex, or food. We will find "enough" only in the God of sufficiency. Our battle isn't really about food but where we go for satisfaction.

In Jesus' teaching in Luke 12, He reminds us that God knows we need food. The Father feeds ravens. They never worry about what to eat. And in Abba's eyes, we are much more important than ordinary birds—He will certainly feed us as well.

And food is a gift. The Father wants us to enjoy His culinary creation of a perfectly ripe peach. To let the juice of the summer watermelon run down our chins. To bite into a Honeycrisp apple and marvel at the perfect blend of sweet and tart. To breathe in the aroma of freshly baked bread and relish every mouthful. Appreciating the Father's good gifts of food is an act of worship.

But God wants to nourish us with more than what will fuel our bodies. He wants to feed us with Himself. The day after Jesus fed five thousand people, some of these fortunate picnickers sought Him out. Because Jesus could see their hearts, He said to them, "Truly, truly, I say to you, you are seeking Me, not because you saw signs, but because you ate your fill of the loaves" (John 6:26). The people saw the miracle of the multiplication of bread, but somehow they did not recognize that the miracle was accomplished by God the Son. It is said that we see only what we are looking for. They weren't seeking God; they were pursuing their next meal.

> The cravings of our bodies are shadows of the yearning of our souls.

I recognize myself in that crowd. How many times have I sought out the Savior only for what He could give me? How many times have I rushed past signs of God working in my life and cared only about the fulfillment of my desires?

But Jesus does not end with a rebuke. He went on to teach the people following Him:

Do not work for the food that perishes, but for the food that endures
to eternal life, which the Son of Man will give to you. For on Him God
the Father has set His seal. . . . Truly, truly, I say to you, it was not
Moses who gave you the bread from heaven, but My Father gives you
the true bread from heaven. For the bread of God is He who comes
down from heaven and gives life to the world. (John 6:27, 32–33)

The people recognized that food that lasted forever was more valuable
than ordinary bread that got moldy in a week. They begged Jesus, "Sir, give
us this bread always" (John 6:34).

And Jesus responded: "I am the bread of life; whoever comes to Me
shall not hunger, and whoever believes in Me shall never thirst" (v. 35).

Jesus Himself is the bread that will satisfy our souls.

Once when I was trying to lose a few pounds, I bought some "diet"
bread. When I made my sandwich with this bread, I immediately saw how
it differed from my usual loaf. The slice of "diet" bread was smaller, thinner.
But the contrast between the loaves was even more apparent when I took
a bite. The new bread was spongier—not as dense, like my favorite whole
wheat loaf. It seemed more like eating air than eating bread. After finishing
the sandwich, I was still hungry.

Too often the things I go after are like that diet bread. Small. Thin. Of
little substance. No wonder they don't fill my heart.

But Jesus is the bread of life—the one thing able to satisfy all my cravings. The one thing that can fill up my empty soul. He is true nourishment—
not some substandard imitation. One of the commentaries I read on John 6
said this:

No matter who it is that comes to Him, he will no more suffer with
hunger, just as he that drinks of the living water of His salvation will
never again be bothered with thirst. To come to Jesus means to believe
in Him as the Savior of the world. All the desires and longings of the
soul find their complete gratification in Him and His mercy.[6]

Jesus promises us absolute satisfaction when we come to Him. Ordinary food sustains our bodies and keeps us alive. Jesus, the true bread from
heaven, nourishes our souls and preserves us for eternal life.

All our longings are meant to lead us to God. The cravings of our bodies
are shadows of the yearning of our souls. God made our bodies to experience

hunger and thirst. But these desires are only faint images of our deepest desires. We were made to yearn for God. Satan will attempt to satisfy us with a seven-course meal or a quick stop at Taco Bell or a glass of wine, but we will never satiate our soul hunger anywhere but in Jesus.

===== GOD'S GRACIOUS FEAST =====

Jesus not only describes Himself as the bread of life, but He also nourishes our souls with His own body and blood. We find Him in the bread and the wine of the Lord's Supper.

> Now as they were eating, Jesus took bread, and after blessing it broke it and gave it to the disciples, and said, "Take, eat; this is My body." And He took a cup, and when He had given thanks He gave it to them, saying, "Drink of it, all of you, for this is My blood of the covenant, which is poured out for many for the forgiveness of sins." (Matthew 26:26–28)

Jesus gave us exactly the food we needed for the nourishment of our faith and the forgiveness of our sins. His words "make eating a morsel of bread and taking a sip of wine a great and gracious feast rather than an empty ceremony."[7] When we eat Christ's body and blood "confidently believing that He was delivered for our offenses and raised for our justification . . . we receive His body and blood, given to us under the bread and wine, as the guarantee of our forgiveness."[8]

Christ's Example

So how can we use our cravings to remind us to go to Jesus? Let's use the example of our Lord.

Jesus Himself was tempted with food. Scripture says, "Jesus, full of the Holy Spirit, returned from the Jordan and was led by the Spirit in the wilderness for forty days, being tempted by the devil. And He ate nothing during those days. And when they were ended, He was hungry" (Luke 4:1–2). Hungry? Try famished. Starving. Ravenous. Satan knew this and urged Jesus to change rocks into bread. The rumbling of Jesus' stomach probably asked the Son of Man to comply, but Jesus did not give in. Instead, He responded with Scripture: "It is written, 'Man shall not live by bread alone'" (v. 4).

What if we did the same? What if we responded to unhealthy cravings for more and more chocolate with a helping of Scripture? What if we filled our souls with God's Word instead of trying to fix the problem with cheesecake?

Keep a few of these Scriptures stored in your pantry.

> For [God] satisfies the longing soul, and the hungry
> soul He fills with good things. (Psalm 107:9)

> The young lions suffer want and hunger; but those
> who seek the LORD lack no good thing. (Psalm 34:10)

> But whoever drinks of the water that I will give him
> will never be thirsty again. The water that I will give
> him will become in him a spring of water welling up
> to eternal life. (John 4:14)

> Because Your steadfast love is better than life, my
> lips will praise You. . . . My soul will be satisfied as
> with fat and rich food, and my mouth will praise
> You with joyful lips. (Psalm 63:3, 5)

When I was a child, my mother used a specific ploy whenever our family was invited to the home of another family for dinner. Evidently, certain relatives had commented on the "healthy" appetites my siblings and I possessed. My mother, not wanting hostesses to have the embarrassment of not having enough food, began doling out fruit before any dinner party. "Here," she would say, "eat a couple of apples before we go." The apples took the edge off our hunger and we were satisfied more quickly at the dinner table.

I think Satan uses a similar strategy. The serpent in the Garden of Eden offered apples (or at least some sort of fruit). But now Satan tempts us with chocolate cake. He points out ice cream and nachos. He steers us toward macaroni and cheese and buttered popcorn. All in an effort to take the edge off our hunger—our hunger for God.

Let's not allow the devil's tactics to fool us. He will constantly attempt to "spoil our appetites" with the things of this world. God invites us to eat and enjoy the good gifts of food He has given us—but to remember that stuffing our stomachs will never truly fill our hearts.

> Let's go to the Bread of Life to satisfy all our longings.

We can't expect one chapter in a book to solve all our struggles with food. If you see yourself in Lee's story or feel like you need more support in this area, I encourage you to seek out nutritionists, dieticians, and wise counselors. Find friends and support groups who will cheer you on in your efforts to change your eating habits.

May we start with the realization that food (or the avoidance of food) will not satisfy our deepest needs. It will never be the "enough" our souls crave. Instead, let's turn to the God of sufficiency when we feel empty. Let's gorge on His Word to satiate our heart-hungers. Let's feast on the Lord's Supper to fill our souls. Let's go to the Bread of Life to satisfy all our longings.

WHAT IS YOUR BIGGEST TAKEAWAY FROM THIS CHAPTER?

O GOD OF SUFFICIENCY,

Thank You for the gift of food. For juicy oranges and creamy avocadoes. For crunchy carrots and sweet treats. You are the giver of all good gifts and sometimes I forget that. Forgive me for taking Your generous provision for granted.

Lord, sometimes I also forget that You are the bread of life—the only one who can truly satisfy my soul. Forgive me for when I try to find what I need in a piece of lasagna or a pound of dark chocolate. You promise that I will never hunger or thirst if I come to You. Thank You for feeding and nourishing my soul. In Jesus' name. Amen.

CHAPTER 5

ENOUGH RELATIONSHIPS

Memory Verse:
Beloved, let us love one another, for love
is from God, and whoever loves has been
born of God and knows God.

1 John 4:7

"I have a problem with holiday movies," I confessed to my friend Linda. "You know the ones—the scenes where the whole big extended family sits around the table. Laughing, smiling people pass around the potatoes and ham. Soft candlelight glows. Every face beams. Movie music begins. As soon as the violins start playing, my tears start flowing—because I can't have that."

You see, I can't have that holiday scene from the movies because my daughter and her family live on the other side of the world, in China. And although my son and his wife live closer, they can't always make the six-hour drive at Christmas. Extended family are spread across the country and are unwilling to come to Chicago in December. (Can't say I blame them.) And as a ministry family, my husband and I can't leave for the holidays.

In fact, this past Christmas Eve, instead of having the whole family around the dining room table, it was only my husband and me. Mind if I cue the violins again and start the pity party?

I know I'm not the only one feeling a deficit in the relationship department. When I speak to groups, lonely women approach me after the sessions and tell me about their longing for a husband—someone to share life with. Others ache to hold children and wonder why it seems God is withholding this blessing. Widows tell of the loneliness of losing their soul mate. Women like me share their own struggles with friendship.

Our need for relationships is real. The triune God created us in His image. He is three persons in one God and so is never lonely. The Father always has the Son and they always enjoy fellowship with the Holy Spirit. So, when God created Adam, He also made a companion for him because He knew, "It is not good that the man should be alone" (Genesis 2:18). God made us for community.

We instinctively know this, so from a young age, we hope for a best friend. We search for a spouse. We make sacrifices to bring children into our families. We join book clubs and Bible study groups. We seek community in churches and volunteer organizations. We spend time connecting with people on Facebook and Instagram.

Yet, often it doesn't feel like enough.

Mr. Right turns out to be all wrong. Family members reject us. Friends desert us when we need them most.

===== PEOPLE WHO NEED PEOPLE =====

Modern science backs up God's statement "It is not good that the man should be alone" (Genesis 2:18). Recent studies show some of the benefits of healthy relationships.

- ◆ Strong relationships may extend your life. One study showed that the risk for premature death increased by 50 percent for those who did not have friends.
- ◆ Friends may keep your mind healthy. A study of Swedish adults age 75 and over found a lower rate of dementia in those with satisfying ties to other people.
- ◆ Strong social ties improve overall health. One study that compared blood pressure, body mass index, and levels of inflammation in the body found those without healthy relationships had worse health.
- ◆ Friends help you through the hard times. Studies have shown that support groups dramatically improve the quality of life for cancer patients.[1]

So make a lunch date with a friend. Call your sister to catch up.

Greed vs. Selflessness

Jesus told the parable of the rich fool in response to a request from a person in the crowd: "Someone in the crowd said to Him, 'Teacher, tell my brother to divide the inheritance with me'" (Luke 12:13). But Jesus refused to enter into that discussion, saying, "Man, who made Me a judge or arbitrator over you?" (v. 14). Instead, He went on to instruct the crowd, "Take care, and be on your guard against all covetousness" (v. 15).

Jesus knew that greed—our constant search for more—can destroy our relationships. The man in the crowd grumbled about his share of the inheritance. We don't know if he wanted more than his fair share or if the brother was withholding what he deserved. In either case, the money of the inheritance was causing a rift in the relationship. A chasm so wide that the man hoped Jesus would step in and settle the dispute.

> The people who possess rich and rewarding friendships are usually the ones with giving hearts.

Greed and selfishness are major contributors to our broken relationships. As a pastor, my husband officiates over many funerals and sometimes witnesses families divided over the money the deceased has left behind. People who got along just fine before the funeral start fighting over who gets the china set and what to do about the vacation cabin. But it doesn't take a death in the family for avarice to destroy marriages, friendships, and family bonds.

How can we find enough in relationships? Perhaps a first step is recognizing where greed has reared its ugly head.

Recognize greed in ourselves. I need to look at my own heart first. Am I acting like the brother who came to Jesus demanding his own way? Where have I been the person who insisted on having more? Have I called on my spouse to come to my aid but grumbled when he needed me to do one small favor? Have I taken friends for granted and been stingy with my time? Have I been tightfisted with forgiveness and held grudges? Have I been sparing with well-deserved compliments while searching for praise for myself? Finding enough in relationships starts with me.

As I contemplated this topic, I realized that the people who possess rich and rewarding friendships are usually the ones with giving hearts. The ones who show up at your doorstep with a casserole when you're recovering from surgery. The ones who send flowers on the anniversary of the death of a loved one. The ones who text you a simple message saying you are in their prayers.

I'm asking God to help me become that kind of person. I pray that He will show me where I have been the one exhibiting greed in my relationships. That He would work the selfless giving nature of Christ in my heart.

Recognize greed in toxic relationships. Part of our journey to "enough" includes eliminating what we don't need. Finding enough in relationships might mean limiting interactions where we are victims of selfishness or greed. Leaving associations where we feel abused. Curbing one-sided friendships.

Certainly, every person has value in God's eyes, and we can't simply toss people aside. But it is helpful to examine our relationships.

Ask yourself questions like these:

- Does this relationship build me up or tear me down? Do I feel encouraged or diminished after spending time with this person?
- Does this relationship make me feel used? Am I always the person who makes sacrifices, or is there give-and-take?
- Is this relationship hurting me? Am I experiencing physical or emotional abuse?
- Does this relationship affirm who I am? Or do I always feel I need to change to please this person?

Obviously, we all have relationships where we need to be the givers. Raising children requires countless sacrifices. Taking care of an elderly parent may mean the ledger of giving is longer on our part. And certainly, there are seasons in marriage and friendship when our giving needs to outweigh what we receive. But where we can expect give-and-take, let's talk with those we love to attain a relationship where both parties feel affirmed and valued.

> True wealth is found in people who love us, care for us, and show up when we're broke.

To find enough in our relationships, we must recognize where greed has crept in and robbed us of meaningful connection and left only bitterness and hurt. While we as loving members of the Body of Christ try to share His compassion with our fallen world, as individuals we cannot survive for long in a relationship with someone who is a black hole of neediness.

Exercising Enough

If you recognize greed in one or more of your current relationships, take action. Most important, if you are in physical danger, leave. Find help at a battered women's shelter. Call the Domestic Violence Hotline.

But if it is safe to do so, confront the person in the toxic relationship. Realize that every person deserves to be treated with respect and compassion. Use "I" statements to communicate your feelings to the other person. For instance, you might say, "When I'm with you, I often feel I'm not good enough. I value our relationship, but I'd appreciate it if you would not constantly tell me how I need to change."

Stuff vs. Relationships

Greed can also affect our relationships when we let our voracity for material wealth overrule our need for meaningful connection with people. Our culture prioritizes money and stuff. These values tempt us to put money ahead of friendship, to spend more time seeking possessions than authentic relationships.

At the end of the movie *It's a Wonderful Life*, Harry Bailey calls his brother George "the richest man in town." I doubt the rich man in Jesus' parable would have agreed with Harry's assessment. By all practical accounting, George had nothing. He owed eight thousand dollars and had no way to pay it. He would certainly lose his business and perhaps his freedom. So how could Harry call him rich? George had wealth in his relationships. His many friends came to the rescue to give him the money needed to fix his cash-flow problems.

My family watches *It's a Wonderful Life* every Christmas, and every year I tear up—even though I know exactly how it ends. My heart melts because deep down, I know it's true. We can't find true wealth in big bank accounts or in stockpiling grain, clothes, shoes, or big-screen TVs. We attain genuine wealth in people who love us, care for us, and show up when we're broke. Friends who make us laugh until our sides ache and who put an arm around us when no laughter can be found. People who hold our hands in hospital waiting rooms and listen to the doubts of our hearts.

The rich man in Jesus' parable stored his surplus grain instead of giving some away. If he had valued people over money, perhaps generosity would have won out over self-preservation. If he had treasured relationships more than possessions, he would have shared rather than hoarded.

In God's kingdom, finding enough means putting others ahead of ourselves.

These practices are not limited to Jesus' stories. Money and stuff often rank higher than people in today's culture. A man may work extra-long hours to gain the promotion and bigger paycheck when all his family wants is a little more of his time. A woman prioritizes her career over relationships and finds herself isolated and lonely. To obtain the bigger house in the desirable neighborhood, both parents work, and the children hunger for their presence. Employment and improving our circumstances are not wrong in and of themselves, but when these displace our vocations as spouse and parent, then we have made them our gods.

I have been guilty of these upside-down priorities. Right now, I have five part-time jobs that consume all my time. Many factors have led to this chaotic state of affairs: I'm a bit of a workaholic. I want to contribute to the family income. I find it hard to say no to worthwhile opportunities. And if I'm honest, I have been influenced by the way society equates our net worth with our self-worth. But while my IRA slowly fills, I've found my heart seems rather empty. I spend too much time in front of my computer and not enough time with people in real life.

To resolve this deficit in my relationship account, I'm starting to make connecting with people a priority. Along with my long list of work-related goals for the next twelve months, one of my chief objectives for this year is to meet a friend for lunch at least once a month. I'm asking God to help me notice the needs of people in my life and to make me willing to abandon my to-do list in order to take a pot of soup to a sick friend or call someone who is grieving. For some of you, this comes naturally, but I admit I might be more like the rich man who stored up stuff instead of giving it away. At times, I may value security more than generosity.

Jesus said, "Greater love has no one than this, that someone lay down his life for his friends" (John 15:13). I may never be called on to die for a friend, but am I willing to lay down my plans? Am I willing to drop my agenda to help someone? Am I willing to give up my time and preferences? In God's kingdom, finding enough means putting others ahead of ourselves.

Exercising Enough

Five Ways to Cultivate Quality Relationships

- **Pray.** Pray for the people already in your life. Pray for new friends. Pray to become a better friend.
- **Carve out time.** Quality relationships require time. Go for a walk with your husband in the evening. Block out an afternoon to spend with your mom.
- **Prioritize face-to-face relationships.** Social media can keep us connected, but it is no substitute for sharing life in person.
- **Be authentic.** Although being real can be scary, honest sharing of our tough stuff deepens relationships.
- **Listen.** Develop the skill of active listening—asking questions, echoing what you heard—to better understand your friend, your spouse, your child.[2]

King Solomon was considered the richest man of his time, but at the end of his life, he realized the futility of his wealth. He said, "Then I considered all that my hands had done and the toil I had expended in doing it, and behold, all was vanity and a striving after wind, and there was nothing to be gained under the sun" (Ecclesiastes 2:11). When he realized his own predisposition to value wealth over people, he observed this tendency in other people as well. He tells a story of a man he observed:

> Again, I saw vanity under the sun: one person who has no other, either son or brother, yet there is no end to all his toil, and his eyes are never satisfied with riches, so that he never asks, "For whom am I toiling and depriving myself of pleasure?" This also is vanity and an unhappy business. (Ecclesiastes 4:7–8)

This man had prioritized work and riches, and yet he was not content. Solomon goes on to say:

> Two are better than one, because they have a good reward for their toil. For if they fall, one will lift up his fellow. But woe to him who is alone when he falls and has not another to lift him up! Again, if two lie together, they keep warm, but how can one keep warm alone? And though a man might prevail against one who is alone, two will withstand him—a threefold cord is not quickly broken. (vv. 9–12)

Solomon discovered that money is never enough but a friend is invaluable. A friend will help you achieve your goals. She will lift you up when you fall and defend you when you feel weak.

Instead of following the example of the man in Ecclesiastes and the rich fool in Luke 12, let's model our lives after Jesus, who ranked relationships with His people over His own comfort. He gave up glory in heaven to be ridiculed on earth. He relinquished gold streets for the dusty roads of Palestine. He left His Father's side to live with us.

Lord, help me to value Your people more than material wealth.

═══ RELATIONSHIPS IN THE BIBLE ═══

The value of human relationships is seen throughout God's Word. Jesus said the commandment to love our neighbor as ourselves is second only to loving God with our heart, soul, mind, and strength (Mark 12:30–31).

The marriage relationship is a picture of the relationship of Christ and the Church (Ephesians 5:25–32). God created Eve because it was not good for the man to be alone (Genesis 2:18) and the family unit was a building block of human society. The Bible contains commandments and instruction on how to be a good child, parent, and spouse.

In Bible times, hospitality was an important cultural value. Most people would extend invitations to travelers—even strangers—to spend a night in their home. The host would provide a meal and food for the traveler's donkey, and would treat the guest as an honored member of the family.[3]

The God of Sufficiency

Recently, two of my best friends moved to be closer to their adult children and grandchildren. (Can you see my envy-green face through the pages?) I'm trying to choose delight in their blessings instead of jealousy. But after the moving trucks pulled away, I was left with loneliness. These were the friends who understood me. The ones who listened without judgment when I poured out my heart. The ones who cried with me when my husband was diagnosed with lymphoma and rejoiced with us when the chemo worked. These women heard all my heartaches, walked with me in seasons of doubt, and consistently pointed me to Jesus. It's not easy to find friends like that.

Ever since these extraordinary women moved, I've been searching for some new friends. What I want is someone who loves me no matter how many times I mess up. Someone who knows me inside and out and yet doesn't reject me. Someone who invites me to the party and always takes time to listen to my list of disappointments. Someone who doesn't try to sugarcoat my frustrations but promises things will get better. Someone who accepts me as I am yet gently challenges me to become a better version of myself.

I start to think, *That's too much to ask. I'll never find anyone like that.* Then I remember—I already have that Someone. God promises to be all those things for me. My dissatisfaction in relationships often comes from looking for the perfect relationship in flawed humans instead of in the God of unfailing love.

We will never find enough in other people. That sounds very depressing and pessimistic, but it's true. And perhaps the less expectation we put on people to fill the void in our hearts, the more fulfillment we will find in human relationships. We need one another, but as flawed individuals, we will frequently mess up and let one another down.

Loving one another well means first receiving God's love.

The only person who will never fail us is Jesus. The only one who will never let us down is God. The Father acts as the perfect dad—even if your earthly parent neglected you. The Holy Spirit constantly comforts you—even when people desert you. Jesus calls you His friend—even when human friends fail you.

This is not to say that life is always easy. Loneliness and isolation can become frequent and unwanted visitors in our lives. At another time in my life when I struggled with a lack of close relationships, I remember I prayed for friends. One day, while reading John 15, I came to verse 15: "No longer do I call you servants, for the servant does not know what his master is doing; but I have called you friends, for all that I have heard from My Father I have made known to you," and God reminded me through these words, "Sharla, You and I are friends. Isn't that enough?" I wish I could say I immediately responded with thankfulness and contentment. But instead I grumble-prayed something like, "Lord, Your friendship means so much to me, but right now I could really use some flesh-and-blood friends." I had grown apart from some people as our circumstances changed. A few friends I counted on disappointed me. And people I reached out to never returned my calls. I felt a little lonely and rejected.

God kept reminding me of His love, and I kept saying, "It's not enough"—until one day when I attended a retreat. The speaker told a rather unremarkable story about attending a banquet with her husband. They arrived early and sat down at an empty table. Soon a young man joined them, wanting to speak with her husband. Next, two couples took seats at the table. These two couples knew each other but hadn't seen each other in a long time. They had a lot of catching up to do. The speaker continued, "Now everyone had someone to talk to except me." She had started feeling sorry for herself when she felt God whisper to her heart, "Aren't I enough for you?"

Immediately, this ordinary story touched my complaining heart. Tears dripped down my cheeks because these were the words God had been speaking to my soul. When I went back to my room at the retreat center, I finally prayed, "Lord, I'm sorry for my refusal to see that You are enough for me. Help me to embrace this lonely period as a time to concentrate on my relationship with You."

Looking back, I see that season of loneliness as a gift from God. The loving Father used the time to teach me to lean on Him for all I needed. He gave me that period to experience Jesus as my "enough." Without it, I might always have tried to find enough in human relationships—and always been disillusioned. I needed a period of earthly loneliness to grow deeper in the relationship that never disappoints.

Prayer Prompt

Write some characteristics you are looking for in a friend. Now write a prayer thanking God for being that friend.

_____

_____

_____

_____

_____

_____

Getting a Refill

As we find our satisfaction in our connection to God, our human relationships can also grow. When God has quenched our need for love, we are better able to give some away. In our home, we use a water purification pitcher to filter chemicals from the water we drink. We can always have pure water—if we remember to refill the pitcher. If I only pour water *out* from the pitcher and never pour more *in*, the container soon becomes empty. There is no pure water to dispense.

In his first epistle, the apostle John reminds us of the importance of receiving in order to give. He wrote:

> Beloved, let us love one another, for love is from God, and whoever loves has been born of God and knows God. Anyone who does not love does not know God, because God is love. In this the love of God was made manifest among us, that God sent His only Son into the world, so that we might live through Him. In this is love, not that we have loved God but that He loved us and sent His Son to be the propitiation for our sins. Beloved, if God so loved us, we also ought to love one another. No one has ever seen God; if we love one another, God abides in us and His love is perfected in us. (1 John 4:7–12)

In this short passage, John reminds us three times to love one another. Certainly our world would be a better place if we all did this. We wouldn't feel a deficit in the relationship department if we all loved one another.

But *how* can we do this? How can we give love away when our own hearts feel empty? We find the key in verse 7: "Beloved, let us love one another, for love is from God."

To become the friend who loves—the one who dispenses encouragement and support like pure water—I have to be filled. To have the ability to love well—giving without expecting anything in return—I need to go to God, who will replenish my heart with His love.

The apostle John seemed especially aware of God's love. Five times in his Gospel, he refers to himself as "the disciple whom Jesus loved" (John 21:20). Perhaps John and Jesus shared a special closeness. Jesus was fully human—maybe Jesus' and John's personalities perfectly suited the other. In modern-day terms, they might have described themselves as soul mates.

But Jesus is also God, and as God, He certainly loved the other disciples just as much. Why didn't each one describe himself as "the disciple whom Jesus loved"? It appears John had a special awareness of the love of God.

This makes me wonder what it might have been like to hang out with John. How did this identity of being loved by Jesus affect his other relationships? Was he the friend you could count on in the middle of the night? the one who generously shared whatever he had? the one who never interrupted your story to tell his own because he never felt the need to prove himself?

Me? I don't always live like I believe I'm "the disciple whom Jesus loved." And when I forget Christ's unfailing love for me, I start trying to refill my pitcher with attention and kudos from others. Instead of giving, I become the needy person who is always taking. I work hard to prove myself—even if it means upstaging someone else. I insist on my own way instead of deferring to my husband. I cling too tightly to friends, making them uncomfortable. I don't take the initiative in starting a friendship because I feel too self-conscious, too unworthy. I operate out of jealousy and selfishness instead of trust and generosity. I'm afraid to be authentic because I'm sure others won't like the real me.

> I needed a period of earthly loneliness to grow deeper in the relationship that never disappoints.

But what would happen if I described myself as "the disciple whom Jesus loved"? How would *your* life look different if you always thought of yourself this way?

I believe that when we rest securely in the love of God who "was made manifest among us," the love that motivated God to send "His only Son into the world, so that we might live through Him" (1 John 4:9), our pitchers are filled. When we relax in His agape love for us as His baptized children, we no longer feel the need to prove ourselves. When we ignore the voices telling us God has forgotten us, we don't need to seek attention from people. We are more able to love each other generously, thoughtfully, even selflessly.

Earthly relationships may continue to disappoint. You may still yearn for a family of your own, for friends you can count on, for someone to share your life with. But remember, even if you receive the man of your dreams or a dozen friends to hang out with, they will never completely meet your needs. Only a true relationship with God can do that.

When I'm resting in God's love for me, I am much more likely to enjoy the people He has brought into my life and much less prone to complain about the relationships I feel are missing. Remember the movie scene I longed for? The one with my family gathered around the holiday table? God gave me that scene in an unexpected way.

A Christian writers group invited me to a retreat in Door County, Wisconsin. I didn't know if I should attend. I didn't know the other writers very well. Would they like me? Would I fit in? Or would I spend the whole weekend feeling uncomfortable and awkward?

Eventually, the need for community won out over fear, and I bravely took a chance. I'm so glad I did. Everyone was warm and welcoming. During the weekend, we took a hike in the woods and shared our writing journeys. We spent time in prayer and in contemplation of God's Word.

One evening two of the women attending prepared a mouthwatering meal of beef short ribs and roasted vegetables. We all sat down at the table (for sixteen!) and enjoyed the feast while talking about our favorite books. At one point in the meal, I looked at the smiling faces glowing in the candlelight and realized God had given me the movie scene I longed for. Not with my biological family, but with sisters in Christ.

HOW WOULD YOUR LIFE LOOK DIFFERENT IF YOU ALWAYS THOUGHT OF YOURSELF AS "THE DISCIPLE WHOM JESUS LOVED"?

I'm still likely to grumble about grandchildren living seven thousand miles away. (If you see me, feel free to stop me if I go on too long.) But I'm finally learning to thank God for what I have: a loving husband, kids who take time to talk to me (even if we have to do it through Skype), and the family of Christ.

Most important, I thank God for being the someone who knows me intimately, loves me as I am, cares for my broken heart, and never gets tired of my desperate need for Him.

WHAT IS YOUR BIGGEST TAKEAWAY FROM THIS CHAPTER?

O GOD OF SUFFICIENCY,

I m grateful for the wonderful people You have brought into my life. Let me never take them for granted but love them with the love You have placed in my heart.

Most of all, thank You for calling me Your friend and being the one who consistently loves me no matter how many times I mess up. The one who listens to my frustrations and is always there for me. The one who invites me to the heavenly party and never rejects me. Help me to remember that I will never find enough in relationships in flawed humans. You are the only person who can truly satisfy.

May I learn to relax in Your agape love so I can be a better spouse, parent, friend. Teach me how to give generously and selflessly as Christ did for me. In Jesus' name. Amen.

CHAPTER 6

ENOUGH TIME

Memory Verse:
And which of you by being anxious can add a single hour to his span of life? If then you are not able to do as small a thing as that, why are you anxious about the rest? Luke 12:25–26

A while ago, I read a story in a music journal about a sixth-grader who came to his weekly piano lesson. The teacher greeted him with "How are things? Anything new?" The earnest young student replied, "Not really, but I wish I could go to the dollar store and buy packages of time. I don't have enough time."[1]

My first reaction to this account was *How sad that a twelve-year-old is already feeling the crunch of time.*

My second thought was *Me too!*

One thing I never seem to have enough of is time. I, too, wish I could zip down to the dollar store and pick up a few bags of extra minutes when I run out of time. Or stock a few jars of hours for when I need more time to practice for Sunday services, craft a blog post, do laundry, cook dinner, write this book . . . Time is a precious commodity—one that always seems to be in short supply. Most of us complain about a lack of time, panic when we're out of time, and frantically tell our friends we have no time.

Although we cannot buy more time, we can be conscious of how we spend it. Every activity, every chore, every interaction requires us to plunk down a bit of the limited currency of minutes, hours, and days we possess.

Like money, we want to use this currency well. But unlike money, we cannot work harder to earn more. I can't even borrow a little of my neighbor's time like the proverbial cup of sugar. I can't stretch it like a pot of chicken soup thinned to accommodate a few unexpected dinner guests.

So, what can we do? How can we ever have enough time? And what does the parable of the rich fool teach us about using this resource well?

Living with an "Eternity Mind-Set"

In Jesus' parable in Luke 12, the rich man frets about storing his abundant goods for the future. But God informs the man of his short-sightedness:

> But God said to him, "Fool! This night your soul is required of you, and the things you have prepared, whose will they be?" (Luke 12:20)

Although the man had a long-range plan, he didn't look ahead far enough. He planned for his time on earth but not for eternity. He didn't have an "eternity mind-set."

I can relate. My husband teases me about being "organizy." I like to plan my days. I make a fresh to-do list each week. I write down new goals at the beginning of each year. I've even been to strategic planning sessions where I've been asked to imagine what I'd like my life to look like in five years and to write long-term objectives.

=== AN ETERNITY MIND-SET ===

Jesus talked about preparing for the future, not by stockpiling possessions and resources for future years on earth but by getting ready for His second coming. After the parable of the rich fool and His reminders of the Father's care, Jesus goes on to urge us all to "be ready, for the Son of Man is coming at an hour you do not expect" (Luke 12:40).

We prepare for this glorious future with Jesus by acting like the faithful manager who obeys his master and follows his instructions even while he is away (vv. 41–48). We practice readiness by relying on the oil of God's grace to keep our faith burning brightly (Matthew 25:1–13).

As we focus on the life we will have in heaven, we live with an "eternity mind-set."

But often these strategies do not consider the time that actually matters—eternity. And I can imagine God speaking to me like He did to the rich fool (although I pray He won't have to use that term with me!): "Sharla, your life on earth is short. Who will get what you worked for? Did you spend your time well? Or did you waste your years on what was not lasting?"

I have difficulty developing an eternity mind-set because my puny mind can't even comprehend "forever." If waiting in line at the grocery store checkout seems endless, how can I possibly grasp the idea of actual time without end?

> Every activity, every chore, every interaction requires us to plunk down a bit of the limited currency of minutes, hours, and days we possess.

Once I contemplated the idea of forever and tried to come up with a representation of eternity. I decided to visualize the difference between our earthly life span and the foreverness of heaven with a little math. To make it easier, I used 100 years to represent life on earth (a long life span) and 1 million years to represent eternity (obviously an inadequate number, but something my mind can sort of comprehend). If 1 inch equals 100 years, how long would 1 million years be? The answer is 278 yards—almost as long as three football fields!

Yet in my everyday life, I direct most of my attention to the one minuscule inch of space. I ignore the other 999,999 inches—the rest of the football fields. Perhaps if I kept my eyes on the end zone and lived with an eternity mind-set, I would use my time more wisely.

I know people who have made conscious choices to use their time for eternity. My husband, for instance, went to college with the intention of becoming a lawyer. But God tugged on his heart. John clearly remembers the moment the numbers on the old-school digital clock in his room flipped over to 11:53 p.m. and he decided to pursue a life of pastoral ministry. But we can't all be professional church workers. So I ask myself, what might it look like to live with an eternity mind-set every day? Perhaps it means serving God in whatever vocation we have. The apostle Paul talked about how our work will impact eternity. He said:

> Whatever you do, work heartily, as for the Lord and not for men,
> knowing that from the Lord you will receive the inheritance as
> your reward. You are serving the Lord Christ. (Colossians 3:23–24)

Whether we are waiting on tables or leading business meetings, wiping noses or selling cars, we do it in service to others because of the Lord's provision for us—that is, because we have an eternal reward. Let's change our viewpoint from working to gain recognition and increasing our bottom line to serving the Lord and glorifying Him, assured of eternal blessings.

Perhaps I can also live with an eternal mind-set with small mindful changes, like not rushing through my daily Bible reading plan in order to get to my "important" work for the day. Or spending less time in front of the computer and more hours with people. Or concentrating less on producing something that will last for only a day, a year, or a decade, and instead focusing more on sharing Christ with my neighbors and pointing them to eternity in heaven.

Living in the Now

God lives in eternity. But He created time. He made the earth turn on its axis, marking days. He designed the moon to circle the earth and the earth to orbit the sun, measuring months and years.

I once heard someone say that God created time because without the division of days, we would become overwhelmed. Perhaps this is true—life without compartments of time might be too enormous for humans to handle. We know the Lord created days and instructed us, "Therefore do not be anxious about tomorrow, for tomorrow will be anxious for itself. Sufficient for the day is its own trouble" (Matthew 6:34).

Yet I rarely pay attention to that advice. I look beyond today and borrow trouble from the future. The man in Jesus' parable took a similar track. He didn't plan for eternity, but he did spend a lot of time and energy planning for his earthly future. When his crops produced plentifully, he thought, "What shall I do, for I have nowhere to store my crops?" (Luke 12:17). Then he said, "I will do this: I will tear down my barns and build larger ones, and there I will store all my grain and my goods. And I will say to my soul, 'Soul, you have ample goods laid up for many years; relax, eat, drink, be merry'" (vv. 18–19). I hear the implication in his words: "When I have enough stored up for many years in the future, *then* I'll be able to enjoy life." He postponed happiness until some indefinite time in the future. But God informed the man he had no future. That very night his life on earth would end.

══ TIME IN THE BIBLE ══

Time in the Near East operated a little differently than our Western customs. While we officially start our day at midnight, the Hebrew day began at sunset and ended at sunset the next day (Leviticus 23:32).[2] In Jesus' day, the practice of dividing the days into hours was a relatively new practice.[3] Jesus met the Samaritan woman at the well at the sixth hour (about noontime) and Mark tells us Jesus died at the ninth hour (3 p.m.).

Each week consisted of six days to work and one day—the Sabbath—to rest. The people of Israel used a lunar calendar corresponding to twelve lunar months. To keep the lunar calendar in sync with the solar year, sometimes an extra month was inserted. Ancient Jews marked the progression of the year with religious festivals. Passover was celebrated in the first month of the year, Nisan (corresponding to our March–April). The Feast of Weeks occurred in the month of Sivan (May–June), and the Day of Atonement happened in Tishri (September–October).[4]

In the French story "The Magic Thread," a young boy named Peter receives a silver ball from an old woman. The old woman tells Peter the silver ball contains a thin golden thread. She explains, "This thread is your life thread. If you don't touch the thread, your life will pass normally. But if you wish to have time pass more quickly, simply pull on the thread a little and an hour will pass by like a minute.

"However," the woman warns him, "use the thread carefully, for once the thread is pulled out, you can never push it back again."

At first, Peter is just happy to have this precious gift and is a little afraid to use it. But one day his arithmetic class seems boring; he gives the thread a tiny pull. Suddenly the school day is over and he is walking the forest path back to his home. After this experience, Peter uses the gift of the magic thread whenever life seems tedious or difficult.

I can find joy when I appreciate the gift of now.

As Peter grows, he continues to tug on the magic thread. He pulls it to hasten his wedding day, hurry along payday, help his children become self-sufficient sooner. He uses the unique gift whenever impatient or annoyed.

Suddenly he awakes to find he is an old man, living all alone.

He searches for the old woman to return the silver ball and ask for a second chance to live his life without it. When he finds her, he thanks her for the wonderful gift. With the magic ball, he has never had to wait or suffer. But life passed by so swiftly that he had no time to fully experience what happened—the good or the bad.[5]

Too often, we are like Peter or like the rich fool, unhappy or dissatisfied with what is happening now. We think, *When I have just that one more thing, then I'll be happy. When I've graduated from school, life will be better. Certainly, marriage will fulfill all my needs. Having children will satisfy all my deepest desires.* Or, *contentment will come once the kids have moved out of the house.*

Like Peter in the French story, I tend to make contentment contingent on some upcoming event, only to find I could have had happiness all along if I had only taken time to engage fully in life. And like the rich man in Jesus' story, I may plan carefully for the future and forget that the future is not guaranteed. But I can find joy when I appreciate the gift of now.

This truth made more sense than ever when my husband found out he had cancer. When the doctors diagnosed John's lymphoma in 2015, they told him, "If you have to get cancer, yours is the type to get." Yet, we knew there was a chance the chemotherapy wouldn't work and my husband would change his address from Illinois to heaven. We both became more aware that this life is short—it can end at any time. I need to live in the present.

Prayer Prompt

Take a minute to write a prayer thanking God for some of the blessings He has placed in your life right now.

_____

_____

_____

_____

_____

_____

_____

_____

I love Psalm 13 because David starts out wishing, like the boy Peter, that all his troubles would be gone:

> How long, O LORD? Will You forget me forever?
>   How long will You hide Your face from me?
> How long must I take counsel in my soul
>   and have sorrow in my heart all the day?
> How long shall my enemy be exalted over me? (vv. 1–2)

David feels like his troubles are overwhelming and God has forgotten him. But he reminds himself of the Lord's unfailing love. Even before the situation is fixed and his enemies are defeated, David finds joy in God's salvation:

> But I have trusted in Your steadfast love;
>   my heart shall rejoice in Your salvation. (v. 5)

We don't have to wait for everything to be perfect to have joy. God will give us joy right now—even before He gives us relief from our problems.

So even though this does not come naturally to this "organizy" person who likes to plan ahead, I'm trying to appreciate now. Instead of postponing happiness until some mythical day when all the tasks on my to-do list are checked off, all my closets are systematized, and all my loved ones are healthy and living within a two-hour drive, I'm learning to look at what is good in life right now and be thankful. Today the sun is shining and the snow is melting. When I got out of the car at the post office, I heard birds singing—a sound I have sorely missed the last three months. At the grocery store, I bought red tomatoes, green grapes, and yellow bananas even though the ground here is still hard and frozen. I can enjoy the aroma of my caramel latte as I open my Bible and read God's Word to me in my own language.

> Whether we are waiting on tables or leading business meetings, wiping noses or selling cars, we do it in service to others because of the Lord's provision for us.

Even in the tough times, I can appreciate the nearness of God as I cry out to Him. I realize more clearly the gift of the important people in my life when it looks like I might lose them. Pain isn't pleasant, but it compels me to lean on God. I don't like struggle, yet I know it intensifies my faith. I don't want to rush past the experiences God has allowed in my life without understanding the tutorial that comes with them.

We don't need to wait for joy. Don't postpone happiness. Enjoy the gift of now.

Exercising Enough

One of my friends asked, "Where does time go?" Often we rush through our days, unaware of how we are spending our precious hours and minutes. The first step in learning to use time well is to determine how you are using it right now. At the beginning of the day, grab a piece of paper and a timer. Set the timer to go off every hour, and when the timer sounds, write what you did during those sixty minutes. At the end of the day, review how you spent your day.

How much time did you spend:

at work? _____

on the internet? _____

with family?_____

with friends? _____

in prayer?_____

reading the Bible? _____

watching TV?_____

doing household tasks? _____

other?_____

other?_____

Was any of this surprising? Are there changes you want to make?

Living in *Chronos* and *Kairos*

But even with an eternity mind-set and learning to live in the present, I often feel I don't have enough time. My tasks, my duties, my responsibilities still outnumber the minutes I have to accomplish them.

I'm not sure why this always happens. Every month I tell myself I will say no to things that don't matter so I will have more time for the things that do. I determine to live focused on God's priorities for my life. My good intentions last for a week or two, then I find myself in the same hectic time crunch. Again, I rush from one activity to the next, feeling stressed and overwhelmed.

Perhaps this occurs because instead of going to the God of sufficiency for reassurance of my worth, I look for signs of significance in my calendar. If I'm honest, I've worshiped at the altar of busyness because a full schedule makes me feel important. After all, constant activity should produce something meaningful, right? In my efforts to accomplish a noteworthy achievement, my life becomes as overstuffed as my sweater drawer. And I wish I could buy more time (and more sweaters!).

Scripture talks about buying time too, although in a very different sense. In the King James Version, Ephesians 5:15–16 says:

See then that ye walk circumspectly, not as fools, but as wise,
Redeeming the time, because the days are evil (emphasis added).

One way to define the word *redeem* is "payment of a price to recover from the power of another, to ransom."[6] We often use the word this way. Jesus redeemed us by paying the price of death to rescue us from the power of hell. But the Greek word translated "redeem" can also have the meaning of "to buy up, to buy up for one's self, for one's use."[7] How can we buy up time? To understand that better, we also need to look at the word *time*.

The Greek language has two words for *time*: *chronos* and *kairos*. *Chronos* is the succession of minutes—measured time. Many of our English words concerning time come from this root: *chronic, chronicle, chronological, synchronized*. *Chronos* is used in Matthew 2:7 when Herod asked the Magi what time the star appeared and in Luke 1:57 when Luke tells us Elizabeth's time to be delivered had come.

Kairos means finding the right time to do something and taking advantage of God-given opportunities.

While *chronos* describes measured time, *kairos* denotes a period of opportunity. It signifies the right time to do something—a set or proper time. Matthew 21:34 uses *kairos* in the parable of the tenants where it says, "The *season* for fruit drew near," and Mark 1:15 uses it when John the Baptist tells the people, "The *time* is fulfilled, and the kingdom of God is at hand" (emphases added). Some experts explain the distinction between the two words by saying *chronos* means the quantity of time and *kairos*, the quality of time.[8] We can envision *chronos* as an atomic clock marking off the nanoseconds that keep slipping away and *kairos* as special, opportune, holy days.

When the apostle Paul told the Ephesians to "redeem the time," he used the word *kairos*. In his commentary on Ephesians, Matthew Henry writes that redeeming the time literally means *"buying the opportunity. It is a metaphor taken from merchants and traders who diligently observe and improve the seasons for merchandise and trade."*[9] Perhaps a good analogy of this is a small business owner who buys crates of strawberries at harvest time, produces jam, and sells the preserves in winter when berries are unavailable. To redeem time in the *kairos* sense doesn't mean purchasing boxes of minutes, but using our days well. It means finding the right time to do something and taking advantage of God-given opportunities.

> We practice *kairos* when we ask God how He wants us to use the time He has given us.

Prayer Prompt

In your own words, define these two terms:
Chronos:

Kairos:

Write a prayer asking God to help you use your *chronos* time in a *kairos* way.

_____

_____

_____

_____

Looking to the God of Sufficiency

When I consider *kairos*, I think of how Jesus, the God of sufficiency, used time. In heaven, the Son of God lived in eternity—without clocks or calendars. But He chose to enter the confines of time for our sake. He came to earth at just the right moment—the *kairos* time—though Old Testament believers most likely felt He had delayed too long.

Jesus practiced *kairos* by reserving time for certain purposes. Jesus filled His days with ministry, yet He always set aside time to pray. Mark tells us that after one particularly busy day of preaching in the synagogue and healing many, Jesus did not sleep in the next day (as I would have after a long day) but got up very early in the morning. He left Peter's house where He had been staying and "went out to a desolate place, and there He prayed" (Mark 1:35). Even though Jesus may have struggled to find a spare hour, He used *kairos* to meet with His Father.

We practice *kairos* when we set aside time to talk to God and listen to Him in His Word. We use God's gift of time well when we spend it with Him.

Jesus also observed the Sabbath. In the Ten Commandments, God prescribed time for the purpose of worship and rest. He told the children of Israel, "Six days you shall labor, and do all your work, but the seventh day is a Sabbath to the LORD your God. On it you shall not do any work" (Exodus 20:9–10). God wanted the seventh day to look completely different from the rest of the week. The Gospels tell us Jesus frequently went to synagogues on the Sabbath. Although He often infuriated the Pharisees by not following all their man-made rules, He followed God's Law. He practiced *kairos* by using the seventh day for worship.

As New Testament Christians, we can practice *kairos* by observing a day of rest and worship. We reserve time for the Lord by reflecting on His Word, worshiping with our brothers and sisters in Christ, and receiving the Lord's Supper.

Jesus practiced *kairos* by making use of opportune moments. When I read the Gospels, I marvel at Jesus' patience and His reaction to interruptions. Once while Jesus was preaching to people in a private home, some men cut a hole in the roof of the house where Jesus was and lowered a paralyzed man to Him through the opening (Mark 2:1–12). (And I get distracted if a cell phone goes off while I'm speaking to a group!) Jesus didn't scold the friends of the paralyzed man for interrupting His sermon, because He knew it was the opportune time to heal this suffering man. It was the *kairos* time to display His healing power and His authority to forgive sins. Another time, Jesus knew

His disciples needed a break, and He said, "Come away by yourselves to a desolate place and rest a while" (Mark 6:31). They didn't get that rest, because thousands of people followed them into the wilderness; and yet Jesus didn't shoo the people away, yelling, "Can't you see we all need a break?" Instead, He had compassion on them and used the *kairos* moment to "teach them many things" (v. 34). It was the perfect time to display His power by supplying a fish dinner for thousands with only a young boy's meager meal.

> God will give me everything I need to do His work—including time.

As a person who likes to manage *chronos* time and schedule events to happen at a certain hour, I balk at interruptions. But God is teaching me that I also need to observe *kairos* time. When a friend experiences a disappointment, it is the opportune time to drop whatever is on my calendar and bring her a loaf of zucchini bread or call her on the phone. When a neighbor grieves a heavy loss, that's the time to demonstrate God's love and share the beauty of the Gospel. When my husband experiences good news, it's time to celebrate! Jesus' life teaches me that interruptions may not be distractions but God-ordained moments to share the blessed truth of the Lord's love and care.

Jesus lived as though His time were not His own. He said, "I have come down from heaven, not to do My own will but the will of Him who sent Me" (John 6:38). In fact, the Book of John records nine times when Jesus talked about doing the work the Father gave Him to do.[10] I imagine there were times when Jesus' human nature wanted to take a day off, ignore the Father's will, and do whatever He pleased. But in His perfect obedience, He focused on His purpose of accomplishing the Father's mission.

We practice *kairos* when we ask God how He wants us to use the time He has given us. We read His Word and discover His priorities—loving Him and loving others, sharing the truth of His grace, practicing forgiveness, patience, and kindness. Conviction pierces my heart because I usually see my time as my own. When I think of someone who uses *kairos* time well, I think of my mother's friend Anne. Even though she is a busy mother of six, Anne takes time to serve many people in her community. Because I live 250 miles from my mom, I'm grateful that Anne regularly visits my mother, calls her often to check on her, and sometimes picks up necessary groceries. My mother was surprised at this woman's kindness, but she was even more astonished when she discovered Anne serves many others in this way. My mother once asked her, "How do you get it all done?" And Anne replied, "God gives every person twenty-four hours each day. We decide how we will use them." I ask myself, *Does my schedule reflect God's priorities?*

MARGIN

Dietrich Bonhoeffer wrote, "We must be ready to allow ourselves to be interrupted by God. God will be constantly crossing our paths and canceling our plans by sending us people with claims and petitions."[11] This is easier to do when we have built margin into our lives. Author Richard Swenson defines margin as "the space between our load and our limits and is related to our reserves and resilience. It is a buffer, a leeway, a gap; the place we go to heal, to relate, to reflect, to recharge our batteries, to focus on the things that matter most."[12]

If we schedule activity for every minute of every day, we panic when we lose the car keys, find ourselves stuck in a traffic jam, or need to stay home with a sick child. No margin means no time to respond to a friend's urgent need. But building a little extra time into our weeks can give the space to call a grieving sister in Christ or visit an unchurched neighbor who especially needs the Good News of Christ after an accident or loss. A few unscheduled hours in our week give us the breathing room to face our everyday mini-crises with peace and calm.

Jesus had enough time. At the end of His ministry, Jesus said, "I glorified You on earth, having accomplished the work that You gave Me to do" (John 17:4). He said this after only three and a half years of ministry, but those few years were enough to complete the work the Father had given Him.

To the world, it may have appeared that Jesus did not use His time well. Jesus' statement of finishing His work would have seemed puzzling to modern-day time-management experts and promotional agents. Perhaps they would have counseled Him, "But You're just getting started! Finally, people recognize Your name. Look at how many people showed up when You rode into Jerusalem. You have to take advantage

> As we practice *kairos* time, we live on God's time—trusting He will give us the hours needed to complete His will and the wisdom to toss all else from our schedules and lives.

of the bump in Your popularity!" His own followers probably still had a long list of things they wanted Him to do. Hundreds of people in Israel still needed healing. Thousands would benefit from a free fish dinner. The whole nation still needed liberation from the pesky Romans.

Exercising Enough

Just like setting limits on possessions can help us curb our consumerism, setting limits on time can aid us in using God's gift wisely. Here are some helpful limits to consider:

♦ **Limit your time on the internet.** Set a timer to prevent you from losing track of time spent surfing the web.

♦ **Limit your number of activities**. Realize you can't do it all. Limit yourself to one activity in each area of your life. For example, one volunteer position at church, one service event in your community, one extracurricular activity for each of your children.

♦ **Limit television.** With cable, dish, and streaming services, the number of television shows and movies available is nearly endless. Pick your favorites and choose the number of hours you will watch each week.

♦ **Limit time spent on household tasks.** Limit the hours you spend on meal preparation (say, thirty minutes a day) or cleaning (two hours per week). Choose simple meals and clean what you can.

What time limit will you use this week?

So how could Jesus declare His work finished? Jesus had not done everything other people wanted Him to do, but He had completed the work the Father had given Him to do. He had enough time to do the Father's will. Mission accomplished.

I'm constantly complaining that I don't have enough time to get everything done. Could it be that unlike Jesus, I am doing things God didn't intend for me? That I've said yes not only to what the Lord wants me to do but to a thousand other little things not meant for me—at least, not in this season of my life? That perhaps, unlike Jesus, I haven't simply worked to bring the Father glory, but have spent many of my precious hours trying to attract attention toward me?

In 2 Corinthians 9:8, I read:

And God is able to make all grace abound to you,
so that having all sufficiency in all things at all times,
you may abound in every good work.

According to this promise, God will give me everything I need to do His work—including time. He will never ask me to do a task and not give me the resources to accomplish it. I find peace in that thought.

And if—no, *when*—I'm feeling I don't have enough time, I can read God's Word and remember that all my hurry and flurry gets me nowhere. Psalm 39:6 says:

Surely a man goes about as a shadow! Surely for nothing they are in turmoil; man heaps up wealth and does not know who will gather!

Recently, I opened up my schedule and invited God in. I repented of worshiping at the altar of busyness and asked the Father for wisdom to see where I've taken on assignments not meant for me. I gave Him veto power over activities and tasks that reflect the world's values instead of His priorities. I want God to help me build margin into my schedule so I can be available to serve others at opportune moments. To show me where to cut the fleeting and temporary to make room for the lasting and eternal.

I'm clinging to God's promise for wisdom (James 1:5) as I dismantle my schedule and put it back together in a *kairos* way. So far, this prayerful process has led me to resign from one of my five part-time jobs because I no longer feel called to this work. I cut back on my tasks in another area of work because the hours spent on those tasks have not proved fruitful. A volunteer position got the axe because my time needs to be focused elsewhere. Now I'm scheduling more time with the people in my life and reserving time to be alone with the Savior. This process will be ongoing, for new opportunities for work will always be available, and new activities will appear enticing.

I have a book on my shelf titled *Secrets to Getting More Done in Less Time*—a book full of useful advice for fitting all our responsibilities into the hours of our days. But maybe the real secret to good time management is doing less. We can't go to the dollar store to buy more minutes, but we can ask God to teach us to redeem the time we have. To make the most of every opportunity. To live with an eternity mind-set. And to rejoice in the gift of the present. As we practice *kairos* time, we live on God's time—trusting He will give us the hours needed to complete His will and the wisdom to toss all else from our schedules and lives.

WHAT IS YOUR BIGGEST TAKEAWAY FROM THIS CHAPTER?

O GOD OF SUFFICIENCY,

Time is a precious gift from You—one that I often squander. I plan my days and weeks but often forget to live with an eternity mind-set. I ignore the gift of now and wait for "someday" to be happy. I live in *chronos* time and miss *kairos* moments. Please forgive me for my misuse of the time You have given.

Help me to redeem the time. May Your Spirit remind me to set aside time to spend with You—in everyday devotional practice and Sabbath worship. Show me how You want me to use the time You have given. There never seems to be enough time for my plans, but I know You will give me what is needed to accomplish Your work. Give me the wisdom to throw out what is unnecessary and distracting from my schedule.

Lord, You created time and will provide what is necessary. In Jesus' name I pray. Amen.

CHAPTER 7

ENOUGH OF ME

Memory Verse:
Consider the ravens: they neither sow nor reap,
they have neither storehouse nor barn, and yet God
feeds them. Of how much more value are you than
the birds! Luke 12:24

I remember the first time I felt I was not enough. That I could never be enough.

I sat at my desk in my eighth-grade classroom, my too-long legs tucked under my chair and my pencil poised over the worksheet the teacher had just assigned. I stared at the question: "What do you want to be when you're finished with school?" I wondered, *Should I write it?* My gut told me I should not be so bold, but I did it anyway. In the blank square of paper, I wrote, "Model."

And immediately regretted it.

The boy sitting next to me—the cute boy all the girls had a crush on—leaned over and stole a look at my paper. His words echoed in the too-quiet classroom: "A model? You? That's a laugh!"

You may also wonder why I had imagined I could have that profession. But you see, just the week before, I had been given a glimmer of hope that I could be someone. All my life I had been the shy, quiet one. The one always chosen last in gym class. The girl who started wearing glasses in third grade. The girl with the strange hairdos. The girl who grew six inches in sixth grade and towered over most of the boys in class.

But the week before the cute boy's comment, the mother of the children I occasionally babysat encouraged me. (I probably looked like someone who needed a little reassurance.) "You know," she said, "when I was your age, I always felt too tall. But when I went to college, I found out height can be an advantage. I earned some extra money for school by modeling. I bet you could do that too."

Which is why I wrote "model" on that eighth-grade worksheet. I was so relieved to discover an upside to my awkward height (pun intended). However, after the cute boy's comment, I realized it was silly to think *I* could be a model. Yes, Mrs. Geweke was tall, but she was also beautiful. Who would hire Old Four Eyes to parade in fashion shows? I was not pretty enough.

I was not enough. Period.

There have been many more times when I didn't feel "enough." When no one asked me to the prom my junior year. When I got a C in Aural Music Theory in college. When I didn't get the teaching job I wanted.

Most of us believe we are not enough. The world, after all, sends constant reminders of this. The mascara commercial tells us we aren't pretty enough. The liposuction ad shouts, "You're not thin enough!" Co-workers may hint we're not smart enough. And most days we tend to agree with all of them.

> I'm tempted to display my importance by wearing the more expensive sweater, buying the bigger house, or boasting about the cooler vacation destination. Because then you'll think I'm enough.

Last year I took a survey of some of the women who read my books and blog posts. I asked, "What topics are you most interested in?" The two most popular topics were finding joy and finding contentment. I then asked, "If you checked the topic of finding contentment, in what areas do you most struggle with having 'enough'?" A few women grappled with enough food and enough success. A few more confessed trouble with having enough stuff or relationships. Almost 20 percent admitted a problem with money. But by far the biggest struggle was "feeling I am not enough"—"good enough" or "pretty enough" or "smart enough." More women checked this box than all the other boxes combined.

Sometimes this seems to be a hidden issue. I look at other people's lives and think they have it all together. The woman with the perfect figure—

certainly she never believes herself defective. The neighbor with all the friends—how could she feel inadequate? The competent boss at work—surely she never considers herself a failure. But me? I'm the inferior one. The unacceptable, unacknowledged, unappealing, unattractive, unfavored, unimportant, unlovable, unmentioned one. And if I've ever doubted it, all I need to do is look on social media to be reminded that I am not enough.

But my little survey uncovered the secret most of us are keeping: we feel that we are not enough.

What does Scripture say about this very personal issue of enough? It tells me two seemingly contradictory statements: you are *not* enough, and you *are* enough. Read on to untangle the apparent discrepancy.

THE QUEST TO BE ENOUGH

Americans constantly strive to be enough. This quest fuels the self-help industry. One research company estimates that $549 million a year is spent on self-help books in America.[1]

The same research company estimated Americans spent $9.9 billion in 2016 on self-improvement books, CDs, seminars, coaching, and stress-management programs.[2]

We keep buying more books, attending more seminars, and listening to more speakers because we feel the need to keep improving ourselves. Not necessarily a bad thing—but God invites us to also remember that in Him we are enough. We can drop the weight of striving.

You Are Not Enough

The rich man in Jesus' parable in Luke 12 amassed possessions and wealth to prepare for the future.

> The land of a rich man produced plentifully, and he thought to himself, "What shall I do, for I have nowhere to store my crops?" And he said, "I will do this: I will tear down my barns and build larger ones, and there I will store all my grain and my goods. And I will say to my soul, 'Soul, you have ample goods laid up for many years; relax, eat, drink, be merry.'" (Luke 12:16–19)

Truth is, I do this too. And I may engage in bigger-barn-building activities not only to prepare for the future; I may store up goods to demonstrate how successful I am. How impressive I am. I'm tempted to display my importance by wearing the more expensive sweater, buying the bigger house, or boasting about the cooler vacation destination. Because then you'll think I'm enough.

However, no matter how big or impressive our barns are, we can never be enough on our own—a fact not easy to accept. It's about as easy to swallow as a weekly serving of liver. But God tells us, "*All* have sinned and fall short of the glory of God" (Romans 3:23, emphasis added), and "There is no one who does not sin" (1 Kings 8:46), and "Surely there is not a righteous man on earth who does good and never sins" (Ecclesiastes 7:20).

I don't want to hear this. I don't grab my bright yellow marker and highlight these verses. Can't I simply ignore these passages?

But I need to listen to God's Word. I can't perform some great and noble deed that will make me worthy of God's love. I can't rationalize my mistakes or make excuses for my sin. No twelve-step self-improvement program can make me good enough to get to heaven.

You Are Enough

Thankfully, God's Word doesn't stop there. Yes, it tells me I can never be enough on my own. But right after the apostle Paul says "for all have sinned and fall short of the glory of God" (Romans 3:23), he continues by saying we "are justified by His grace as a gift, through the redemption that is in Christ Jesus, whom God put forward as a propitiation by His blood, to be received by faith" (vv. 24–25). All those big, churchy words tell me that because of Jesus' blood spilled on the cross, the Father pronounces me righteous. God knew we could never be enough, so He sent Jesus. Therefore:

The world sends us constant reminders that we are not enough.

God declares I am enough in Christ.

Because of this truth, I can rejoice in the seemingly bad news that I can never be enough on my own. I can give up my quest for perfection. This doesn't mean I can't have any goals or ambitions, but I can lay down the burdens of attempting to be good enough, successful enough, important enough. I can relax—absolutely assured that in Christ, I am righteous in God's eyes.

Prayer Prompt

Thank God that Jesus is enough so you don't have to be.

_____

_____

_____

_____

_____

_____

_____

This seems almost unbelievable—but wait, there's more. Not only does God declare me enough, but He also sees me as valuable and precious. Right after the parable of the rich fool, Jesus says, "Consider the ravens: they neither sow nor reap, they have neither storehouse nor barn, and yet God feeds them. Of how much more value are you than the birds!" (Luke 12:24).

In a similar passage in Matthew, Jesus tells the disciples that, yes, there will be tough times. Sometimes people won't listen to them. Instead, people will persecute them and call them names. But the disciples are not to confuse the world's assessment of their worth with the Father's appraisal. He tells them not to worry about the judgment of others and reassures them of their value:

> Are not two sparrows sold for a penny? And not one of them
> will fall to the ground apart from your Father. But even the hairs
> of your head are all numbered. Fear not, therefore; you are of
> more value than many sparrows. (Matthew 10:29–31)

Jesus tells the disciples and me, "Fear not." Yet how often I do just that! I fear because I don't have an impressive job title. I worry my work is insignificant. I'm terrified my life won't matter.

But my fear is unnecessary if I rest my worth in God's opinion of me. He reassures me that I have more value than many sparrows—birds God keeps a close eye on. The Father knows me so well, He even numbers the hairs on my head. (Was it number 10,981 that came out in the brush this morning?)

God notices me. Values me. Loves me.

Sometimes I have trouble believing this. How can God love me just because He loves me? How can He value me if I can't demonstrate my worth?

I remember confessing this to my friend Gail a couple of years ago. Over spinach omelets and toast, I dared to say out loud what had been rolling around in my thoughts and prayers. "I realized something the other day," I began. "Deep down, I don't believe I'm valuable without achieving something important or significant. Intellectually, of course, I know there is nothing I can do to earn God's love. But inside, I wonder, *How could this be true?* I feel I need to prove my worth."

> There is nothing I can do to make God love me more than He already does.

My way of garnering attention has always been through accomplishment. Maybe you got the spotlight because of your beauty, your talent, or your comic wit. I had none of those things but was a pretty good student, so I pursued attention from my parents and teachers through good grades. I studied my way to becoming valedictorian of my high school class. Somehow this led me to believe that if I worked hard enough, I could be someone important someday. So I pushed myself. Set goals. Achieved advanced degrees. Wrote a couple of books. Volunteered with community organizations. But I didn't feel I had accomplished anything significant. And I wondered, *Is God disappointed with me?*

But God's Word reassures me that He values me—period. And because of that, I was ready to toss out my crippling beliefs. Somehow, admitting them to my friend Gail helped me see them for what they were. I went home and wrote in my journal:

> *I hear God speaking to me that my perspective on grading myself on my performance is enslaving me. That it's a sin because I want glory for myself, not God, because it trivializes Jesus' sacrifice; because personal achievement has become an idol—something I place above God's acceptance of me.*
>
> *Lord, I confess my sin. I want to be free of the shackles. I'm sorry for wanting glory for myself, for placing more value on worldly recognition than on Your love; for thinking I would be more important to You if I accomplished more for You—when Jesus has already done everything necessary and there is nothing I can do to make You love me more.*

Prayer Prompt

Lord, I see I've been stuck in the chains of:

_____

_____

_____

_____

Thank You for Your grace, which releases me from these shackles. Help me to live free in Your:

_____

_____

_____

I'm hoping you will read this and give me grace—not only for my run-on sentences, but for my obvious failures. In my pride, I thought my accomplishments would make me more valuable, but in the process I made Christ's work seem less essential.

> Jesus invites us to rest in His enoughness and live for His glory.

I know I'm not the only one who struggles in this area. Just last night I was tucked into bed reading *Fiercehearted*. Author Holley Gerth admits:

> I thought if I did get a tattoo, it would say, "By grace alone." Because it's the truth I most need to remember and most often forget. I have been a grace-plus girl. Grace plus my efforts. Grace plus my goodness. Grace plus my trying. All those pluses only subtract from what Jesus is freely giving me. What has already been mine for so very long.[3]

I pray that if you have also been a grace-plus girl, if you've worn the chains of personal achievement, that you will find freedom in the truth that Jesus has already done everything necessary for your approval before God. You can let go of striving for recognition and drop the weight of personal glory. You can stop trying so hard. In Jesus, you are already enough.

═══ HOLY SPIRIT HOLES ═══

In the Middle Ages, Christian churches painted heavenly scenes on their great vaulted ceilings, which also disguised trap doors. At the Feast of Pentecost, these doors were opened, and doves were released into the sanctuary through them. These holes became known as "Holy Spirit holes."[4]

We need Holy Spirit holes in our hearts where God can empty us of ourselves and fill us with the grace and mercy of Jesus. Our pride and striving can keep these doors tightly shut. But when we allow God to empty us of our need to prove ourselves, we can be filled with God's miraculous and unearned love.

═══════

Enough in the Ordinary

A few years ago, I attended a writing conference where one of the speakers asked participants to write the titles of our three favorite movies. It didn't take me long to come up with three: *While You Were Sleeping*, *It's a Wonderful Life*, and *The Sound of Music*.

"Next," the speaker said, "think of something these movies have in common. What ties them together? What underlying theme do you find in all three? This is a clue to your true passion."

It took me much longer to uncover a shared theme. After all, what do a Chicago token taker, a small-town loan officer, and an Austrian nun have in common? Finally, I realized all three movies have a main character who thinks he or she desperately wants one thing, but in the end discovers happiness in something totally different.

Yes, I thought, *this reflects my passion of living in the love of Jesus.* Time and again my human nature desires something out of my reach. I become certain contentment is not possible without this one thing. Sometimes God answers my prayers by giving me what I desire, but more often He gently and lovingly shows me that what I long for doesn't lead to joy. I reluctantly give up the dream, plan, or goal, and God gives me something much more satisfying in its place.

But recently, I realized another connective theme among the three movies. During the period of time when I finally recognized the idol of accomplishment in my life, I saw the theme of . . . ordinary. At the beginning of each movie, the characters—Lucy Moderatz, George Bailey, and Maria Von

Trapp—want something extraordinary, glamorous, or special. But at the end, they find fulfillment of their dreams in the commonplace, mundane, and ordinary. In *While You Were Sleeping*, Lucy has a crush on a handsome, mysterious, successful businessman but finds happiness with his more humble tradesman brother. George Bailey dreams of traveling the world and building impressive skyscrapers but discovers his life has impacted hundreds of people while he stayed in his humdrum hometown and worked at the family business. Maria thinks she needs to serve God through full-time Christian work and retreating from the everyday world, but God calls her to a more ordinary role of wife and mother. (This movie has a little twist: Maria's life turns out to be extraordinary—even as she chooses the ordinary path.)

This is not easy for me to admit, but I have been like Lucy, like George, like Maria. I wanted to do something big for God—write a best seller or lead hundreds of people to Christ. I wanted to impress the world and show God I deserve His love and grace. Perhaps this is because our culture continually drums this call to big and important. A truck commercial that frequently plays on my TV goes something like this:

How do you want to live? As a decent person? fine human being? good father? friend? son? Is that it? Good? Of course not.

Parent of the year? Better. Employee of the month? Absolutely. One of a kind. The center of their world. Like a boss. Like a pro.[5]

As the truck rolls across the screen, the ad reminds me it is not enough to be good, to be decent, to be a fine human being. I need to be better or the best.

But God doesn't call me to do something big and important. He asks me to love the people around me and work in the place where I find myself. This may not look impressive or get my name on the five-o'clock news. My seemingly insignificant efforts may not win awards or garner a million hits on social media. But as I obey in the small things, God Himself will do the extraordinary.

Even Jesus' disciples had trouble understanding that in God's kingdom, less is more and ordinary is extraordinary. While walking in Galilee one day, Jesus' twelve closest followers were caught discussing which one of them was the greatest. Jesus called them on it and then gave them the key to true significance: "If anyone would be first, he must be last of all and servant of all" (Mark 9:35).

I'm certain this is not what they wanted to hear. Greatness comes through service? Importance is achieved by coming in last? Prominence is a result of blending into the woodwork? They might have thought the truck commercial made more sense.

Oswald Chambers, author of the devotional *My Utmost for His Highest*, wrote:

> It is ingrained in us that we have to do exceptional things for God—but we do not. We have to be exceptional in the ordinary things of life, and holy on the ordinary streets, among ordinary people—and this is not learned in five minutes.[6]

God calls us to the ordinary. He calls us to everyday faithfulness. He calls us to adopt the words of John the Baptist, "He [Jesus] must increase, but I must decrease" (John 3:30). At first, this seems a hard thing. We want to be noticed. We want to be special.

But constantly striving to prove ourselves is exhausting. Jesus invites us to rest in His enoughness and live for *His* glory. As we focus on decreasing, we let go of pushing toward the exceptional and remarkable. We live redeemed and restored lives that are anything but ordinary because the Spirit dwells within us. We become less noticed, but Jesus' fame grows.

Getting Ahead

How might a modern self-help book finish this sentence?

"If anyone would be first, she must _____

_____."

How did Jesus finish this sentence?

"If anyone would be first, he must _____

_____" (Mark 9:35).

Which advice do you follow most often?

_____

_____

_____

_____

The God of Sufficiency

Jesus is enough. Jesus has made *you* enough. So how can we connect to the God of sufficiency and grasp these truths?

One of the ways I have embraced these truths is by praying an ancient prayer. I first discovered the prayer when I began exploring spiritual disciplines. Several books on Christian spirituality described the practice of repeating this one supplication hour by hour. A couple of friends told me how praying this short-as-breath prayer throughout the day kept their thoughts centered on Christ. But somehow, I couldn't work up any enthusiasm for this prayer:

"Lord Jesus Christ, Son of David, have mercy on me, a sinner."

Truth be told, I didn't like reminding myself that I am a sinner. I didn't want to rehearse the ways I had fallen short of God's requirements. I didn't want to remember the ways I had broken His commandments. The prayer seemed anything but comforting.

Exercising Enough

Write the prayer, "Lord Jesus Christ, Son of David, have mercy on me, a sinner" on a 3 x 5 card and carry it with you throughout the day. Or post it in a prominent place. Whisper this prayer often in the small moments of your day. At the end of the day, write your heart's reaction to this petition. How did it make you feel?

_____

_____

_____

_____

Did those feelings change throughout the day? Did praying this petition draw you closer to God?

_____

_____

_____

_____

My research on Christian spirituality showed that this ancient prayer is derived from the words of blind Bartimaeus in Mark 10:47: "And when he heard that it was Jesus of Nazareth, he began to cry out and say, 'Jesus, Son of David, have mercy on me!'" They also echo the words of the tax collector in Jesus' parable in Luke 18:

> He also told this parable to some who trusted in themselves that they were righteous, and treated others with contempt: "Two men went up into the temple to pray, one a Pharisee and the other a tax collector. The Pharisee, standing by himself, prayed thus: 'God, I thank You that I am not like other men, extortioners, unjust, adulterers, or even like this tax collector. I fast twice a week; I give tithes of all that I get.' But the tax collector, standing far off, would not even lift up his eyes to heaven, but beat his breast, saying, 'God, be merciful to me, a sinner!' I tell you, this man went down to his house justified, rather than the other. For everyone who exalts himself will be humbled, but the one who humbles himself will be exalted." (vv. 9–14)

Right away I notice that Jesus told the story about the tax collector and Pharisee to "some who trusted in themselves that they were righteous" (v. 9). Hmm. It seems this parable might be directed at me—someone who desperately wants to prove her worth. Someone attempting to be enough on her own. The truths of this parable speak as loudly to me as they did to the Pharisees of Jesus' day.

I cannot find "enough" through comparison. The Pharisee opened his prayer with "God, I thank You that I am not like other men, extortioners, unjust, adulterers, or even like this tax collector" (v. 11). This man believed he had God's favor because he behaved better than other people.

I, too, tend to compare myself with others. This usually results in one of two things. Evaluating myself against "bad" people, like the Pharisee did, leads to thoughts of pride: *I'm not so bad. I'm capable. I'm worthwhile.* But looking at people more beautiful, more fit, or more successful unleashes feelings of failure. *I'm nothing. I'm a disappointment. I'm definitely not good enough.* Neither option draws me closer to the God of sufficiency. I'm staring at myself, not my loving Father.

I can't find "enough" through personal achievement. The Pharisee in the parable continued, "I fast twice a week; I give tithes of all that I get" (v. 12). He told God, "See all that I do!" He thought his spiritual accomplishments made him enough in God's eyes.

I have already told you about my struggles in this area. The manufacture of my chains of personal achievement began in my early years. I constantly strove for attention through A's on my report card, academic honors, and kudos from teachers.

Perhaps this spilled over into my relationship with God. Like the Pharisee—who in effect was saying, "I deserve an A in fasting and tithing, and my report card should read, 'Righteous and Approved'"—I was trying to prove myself to God by getting all A's in Bible study, prayer, and "Doing Something Important for God."

But I can never find approval through impressive rankings. I can never earn grades high enough to demonstrate my worth to God.

PHARISEES AND TAX COLLECTORS

The Pharisees were a prominent Jewish sect, consisting of Jewish authorities and strict observers and teachers of the Torah. They were not a part of the government, but because they were a large group and very popular with the common people, they possessed power.[7]

The Pharisees believed the Jews needed to separate themselves from Gentiles in order to live as the people of God. So they strictly observed Moses' Law, which contained the Ten Commandments and a total of 613 laws. However, the Pharisees created thousands of other laws designed to clarify the original 613, making following God's Law a heavy burden.[8] For instance, the Law of Moses prescribed a fast one day a year on the Day of Atonement, but the Pharisees fasted *two* days every *week*.[9]

Jesus criticized the Pharisees because they made the outward appearance of following the Law more important than inward righteousness and devotion to God (Matthew 23).

Tax collectors in Jesus' day were not the most popular people in town. Not only did they hound people for what they owed the government, but they also often collected a hefty surcharge for themselves. The Roman government gave the right to collect taxes to the highest bidder, and it allowed local tax gatherers to levy an extra percentage for themselves. These tax officials were generally considered dishonest collaborators with the hated Roman government.[10]

I find "enough" by acknowledging my need for God. After the Pharisee's prayer, Jesus described the tax collector: "But the tax collector, standing far off, would not even lift up his eyes to heaven, but beat his breast, saying, 'God, be merciful to me, a sinner!'" (Luke 18:13). The tax collector didn't try to prove himself by reciting his above-average grades in giving and religious practices. He simply confessed his sin. And Jesus said, "I tell you, this man went down to his house justified, rather than the other" (v. 14). God's approval comes when I admit I am not enough.

In God's upside-down kingdom, "Everyone who exalts himself will be humbled, but the one who humbles himself will be exalted" (v. 14). The one who tries to prove he is enough will not get God's approval. But the one who admits he is not enough—the one who acknowledges his need for mercy—is the one who receives justification in God's eyes.

This became a reality when I finally tried praying that ancient prayer. In small moments of the day, I whispered, "Lord Jesus Christ, Son of David, have mercy on me, a sinner." Instead of bristling against the reminder of my failures, my mistakes, my not-enoughness, the prayer helped me remember my desperate need for God's mercy. It reminded me that God doesn't give me this grace because I deserve it. This understanding frees me from a life of striving for an imaginary A+ grade in prayer or an "Outstanding" comment on my Christian service. Praying this prayer releases me from a life of performance. I receive God's grace as the gift it is.

Exercising Enough

How do you try to get the spotlight? Is it your appearance? intellect? athletic ability? accomplishment? sharp sense of humor? Write some of the ways you attempt to be enough.

_____

_____

God has given us gifts of beauty, skill, and talent. But we are to use them for His glory and not our own. Write a prayer thanking God for the gifts He has given. Confess any sin of using His gifts for your own glory instead of His. And thank Him that He is constantly noticing you and loving you, even when the world seems to ignore you.

Psalm 46:10 says, "Cease *striving* and know that I am God" (NASB). I have been striving so long, I'm not sure I know what it is like to not push myself, try harder, struggle to be enough. But in the story of the Pharisee and tax collector, God teaches me that I need to let go of my pride and the mistaken idea that I can be enough by working harder. He invites me to find rest through faith in Christ's death and resurrection. He reassures me that satisfactory marks in God's book come through admitting my sin and my need for mercy.

Take this truth and tuck it into your soul:

I don't have to strive to be enough, because in Jesus I already am.

And whenever you feel the need to achieve to get on God's good side or perform to have a spot on some imaginary list of notable Christians, pray that ancient prayer, "Lord Jesus Christ, Son of David, have mercy on me, a sinner." Release the need to prove yourself, because it can't be done. Receive God's generous and freely given gift of grace. As we dwell in God's mercy, we learn how to live our beautiful, ordinary, everyday lives in freedom.

WHAT IS YOUR BIGGEST TAKEAWAY FROM THIS CHAPTER?

O GOD OF SUFFICIENCY,

I long to be enough. The world constantly reminds me of my faults and inadequacies. Too often, I listen.

For a long time I've allowed the shackles of perfectionism and performance to enslave me. Only Your grace unlocks the chains, reminding me that it is not what I do but what Christ has already done that makes me enough. I no longer need to strive for fame and recognition or honor and acclaim.

Help me to rest in Your love and grace. To notice You in my ordinary, mundane days. To serve out of a desire for Your glory instead of mine. In Jesus' name. Amen.

CHAPTER 8

ENOUGH FOR NOW

Memory Verse:
For all the nations of the world seek after these things, and your Father knows that you need them. Instead, seek His kingdom, and these things will be added to you. Luke 12:30–31

A woman had a prosperous business that produced an adequate income. She acquired a large home with plenty of storage space for her many belongings. Using her killer bargain-hunting skills, she filled her closets with fashions, her cupboards with dishes, and her many, many bookcases with books.

This woman had a family who loved her and friends who supported her. She had work she enjoyed and adequate free time to travel to beautiful and fascinating destinations. Yet somehow it wasn't enough.

After one particularly successful shopping session, she came home with more fashion finds than would fit in her current closet space.

"What should I do?" she fretted. "I don't have room for all my beautiful clothes." Then she said, "I know! I'll build new and bigger closets. Maybe I'll even call the Closet Experts and convert a spare bedroom into a custom storage space for all my fashions. I'll have them build racks for pants and rods for tops. I'll design drawers for sweaters and shelves for shoes. Then I'll sit back and say to myself, 'Now you have enough to be fashionable for years to come. You can finally be content.'"

But God interrupted her strategies for sweater storage with the announcement she would no longer need any of her fabulous fashion finds. Her earthly life was over.

You might recognize this as a retelling of the parable of the rich fool. We've examined this story from multiple angles, but this is how I imagine Jesus might tell the parable today—especially if I were in the crowd.

Honestly, even if this woman (whoever she might be) could complete her custom closet and stock it with all of her favorite styles, satisfaction would remain elusive. Maybe happiness would visit her heart and home for a while. She might smile every morning for a week as she entered the perfectly organized space to choose the outfit of the day. Perhaps she would take every opportunity to show off the closet to her fashion-minded friends.

But soon the old dissatisfaction would resurface. A new desire would pop up. A different "must-have" would emerge.

How do I know? Because my real life resembles that parable. No, I don't have a room-size closet, but the closet I do have is spacious and full of clothes. (Recall the forty-seven T-shirts I told you about in chapter 3?) I have a loving family, fabulous friends, work I enjoy, the money and time to travel—and I still complain that I don't have enough.

Like the rich fool who told himself he could sit back and relax, eat, drink, and be merry when he had enough stored in his barns, I have been sure that happiness would arrive when I obtained a new outfit, achieved the next goal, or took a real vacation. And yes, contentment entered my life when I experienced those things, but somehow it never stayed long. Soon satisfaction simply got up and walked out the back door.

ARRIVAL FALLACY

Often we believe reaching a financial goal or finishing a big work project or getting the dream kitchen we've always wanted will bring satisfaction. Unfortunately, just as often we become disillusioned when achieving the goal doesn't bring the happiness we envisioned.

We tell ourselves, "I'll be happy as soon as . . . ." But this turns out to be a myth. It's called "arrival fallacy"—the false belief that arriving at a desired destination will ensure happiness.

Psychologists explain it is not wrong to pursue goals or seek self-improvement. The problem lies in expecting the accomplishment of the goal to deliver contentment, when it is actually the journey toward the objective that gives life meaning and purpose.[1]

So set that goal, establish an objective, focus on a target, but enjoy the journey.

Perhaps you, too, ask yourself, "Why can't I learn contentment?" Most of us struggle to hang on to the satisfaction we desire. It might surprise you to know there is even a name for the phenomenon of fading happiness. Psychologists call it "hedonic adaptation." This concept describes the fact that no matter how wonderful something new makes us feel, we will eventually coast down the hill of our ecstatic high to an emotional set point.

Scientists propose that hedonic adaptation happens because when you first get a long-desired item or reach a long-pursued goal, a lot of positive events take place. At the start of the desired job, you revel in the new challenges, the bigger office, the fatter paycheck. But after a while, you become accustomed to these changes; you may not even notice them anymore. The excitement and happiness that were present when you first shook hands with your new boss fade and you start looking for the next obsession to give you that same positive high.[2]

> Contentment entered my life when I obtained a new outfit or achieved the next goal, but somehow it never stayed long. Soon satisfaction simply got up and walked out the back door.

The Bible has a term for this phenomenon too. Paul tells the Ephesians that they "were taught in Him, as the truth is in Jesus, to put off your old self, which belongs to your former manner of life and is corrupt through *deceitful desires*" (Ephesians 4:21–22, emphasis added). Deceitful desires—misleading and deluding wishes, wants, and cravings—are part of our sinful nature. As fallen human beings, we tend to believe the next promotion, achievement, or designer handbag is the missing ingredient to our happiness. When that doesn't happen or the enjoyment doesn't last, we feel deceived, duped, and double-crossed.

However, Paul goes on to say that we, as Christians, are renewed in the spirit of our minds (v. 23) and that we have "put on the new self, created after the likeness of God in true righteousness and holiness" (v. 24). And I think, *I've known Christ a long time. Shouldn't I recognize a deceitful desire by now? Shouldn't I be a little farther down the road to contentment?*

A Holy Longing

Then I read something that helped me realize why I struggle with satisfaction, why true contentment is not available here on earth. Augustine of Hippo, an Early Church Father, wrote:

"The whole life of the good Christian is a holy longing."[3]

Suddenly everything made sense. We can never experience total satisfaction here on earth. In our hearts, we will always long for more because we were created for more than this fallen world. No matter how big our houses, how much success we enjoy, or how much money we have in the bank, we will naturally want more. While all of these things have the potential for good in our lives, they can't truly satisfy.

It's stated this way in 2 Corinthians 5:2: "For in this tent we groan, longing to put on our heavenly dwelling." In this life, we moan and groan because whatever we have now—whether a tiny studio apartment or a thirteen-room mansion—it simply cannot quench our longings. Rice and beans or lobster and caviar, obscurity or fame—they all come short of satisfying the ache in our hearts.

> "The whole life of the good Christian is a holy longing."
>
> Augustine of Hippo

When John and I travel to see our daughter and her family, the trip requires two or three flights with layovers in noisy airports, plus a three-hour car ride to get to their home in China. After thirty to thirty-five hours of travel, we want nothing more than to find a horizontal position and rest. But even though exhaustion reigns, our bodies may resist sleep. China is thirteen hours ahead of Chicago time. Night and day, light and dark are completely reversed. During most of the visit in China, we feel tired and sleepy during daylight hours but wide awake in the middle of the night when we want to sleep. Our bodies are tuned to one time zone, and they struggle to function in another.

We experience something similar in our spiritual life. God designed our souls for heaven, and they struggle to function here on earth. We shouldn't expect this life to be adequate or satisfying. King Solomon wrote this truth—that God "has put eternity into man's heart" (Ecclesiastes 3:11). Our hearts are on heaven's time zone, and no striving or effort will ever make this fallen world's environment completely comfortable.

What gain has the worker from his toil? I have seen the business that God has given to the children of man to be busy with. He has made everything beautiful in its time. Also, He has put eternity into man's heart, yet so that he cannot find out what God has done from the beginning to the end. I perceived that there is nothing better for them than to be joyful and to do good as long as they live; also that everyone should eat and drink and take pleasure in all his toil—this is God's gift to man. (Ecclesiastes 3:9–13)

So what can we do? How can we learn contentment? Even though we can't expect this life on earth to satisfy our souls, we can learn to live with enough for *now*.

Worship the God of Sufficiency

My daughter has lived in China so long that she has become accustomed to China time. She can also speak the language and has adapted to sights and sounds we find so strange. However, she misses certain comforts of home. One thing she cannot adapt to is Chinese chocolate. Chocolate candy made in China typically contains so much wax that one of my daughter's friends commented, "I've tasted better candles." Perhaps Chinese residents have never tasted the good stuff, but once you have let a creamy dark chocolate melt on your tongue, the cheap, waxy stuff simply won't do.

The same is true for our spiritual lives. Before knowing the triune God, we may be satisfied with what this world offers because we don't know anything better is available. But once God reaches down to us and we receive the redemption Christ offers, we experience a joy like never before.

However, we—as forgetful and wayward humans—may forget this true source of joy. We may search for happiness here on earth and wonder why this bland version of life doesn't satisfy.

That is why God reminds me, "Delight yourself in the LORD, and He will give you the desires of your heart" (Psalm 37:4). As I delight in God—telling Him my longings for His love—my other desires are recalibrated. Like real chocolate that delights my tongue, I "taste and see that the LORD is good" (Psalm 34:8), and I realize that all the cheap imitations and substandard flavors of life I've used to satisfy my cravings will never work.

I delight in God by worshiping Him. As I worship the Lord, I find the source of fulfillment, and my yearnings are stilled. He refocuses my desires and I find joy.

131

Thomas à Kempis prayed:

There is nothing created that can fully satisfy my desires. Make me one with You in a sure bond of heavenly love, for You alone are sufficient to Your lover, and without You all things are vain and of no substance.[4]

Prayer Prompt

Turn Psalm 37:4, "Delight yourself in the LORD, and He will give you the desires of your heart," into a prayer. Worship God by telling Him how much you delight in Him. Mention specific characteristics of God that give you joy. Here are a few to get you started: **His faithfulness, His caring heart, and His goodness.**

_____

_____

_____

_____

_____

_____

_____

_____

Give God Your List

Although I appreciate the opportunity to visit my daughter, son-in-law, and grandkids in China, I really hope that sometime soon they will return to the States. (And maybe live next door?) When they first moved seven thousand miles away, I constantly complained to God. Contentment had not only stepped out the back door but traveled to the other side of the world.

We've already examined Psalm 37:4:

Delight yourself in the LORD, and He will give you the desires of your heart.

Having my family close is definitely one of the desires of my heart. It's close to the top of my prayer list. So I keep reminding God of His promise in verse 4 of Psalm 37. But then the Holy Spirit points to verse 3:

Trust in the LORD, and do good; dwell in the land and befriend faithfulness.

God promises to give me the desires of my heart, but first He asks me to *trust* Him.

Lately I've discovered that when I struggle to trust God, I need to go to Him in honesty. When I'm distracted by things I want, I can stuff those desires down because they're not spiritual. I can avoid praying about them because they don't seem like something God would care about.

But of course, God knows the desires of my heart anyway. So the best thing I can do is bring my whole wish list to Him. Even if the list has things that seem trivial or impossible, when I talk to God about them, He can help me sort them out.

> As I delight in God—telling Him my longings for His love—my other desires are recalibrated.

I don't simply pray God will give me everything on my list. *I give Him the list.* In releasing my inventory of desires, I affirm trust in the Father's love, confidence in His wisdom, and faith that He will answer my prayers when the time is right.

The Father tells us that He hears all our prayers (Micah 7:7) and invites us to pray with all kinds of requests (Ephesians 6:18). So I bring my prayers—big and small—into God's presence, trusting His will.

Exercising Enough

Write out a list of your desires—everything you long for, even if some of them seem unspiritual or trivial. Pray over each item. Then give God the list, trusting Him to give you what is good.

_____

_____

_____

_____

_____

God still hasn't answered my prayer to have my family close, but He has given me peace in the current circumstances. I thank God for the blessings of Skype and airplanes and email that help us stay close over the miles.

When I tell my gracious heavenly Father I'm ready to trust Him, my heart changes. When I give God my desires, they lose their grip on my soul.

Live with Anticipation

Part of the fun of going to China is anticipating the journey. During the months leading up to our trip, we make our travel plans, book our flights, and look online for amazing things to see when we get there. Our daughter sends us lists of things to bring along—things she can't get in China, like shoes in her size, oregano, and, yes, chocolate. When we Skype, the grand-kids tell us about all the games they want to play when we arrive. We look forward to the hugs not available through email and the heart-to-heart conversations not possible on Skype. We can hardly wait to get to China, but even before we arrive, we experience the joy of looking forward.

Psychologists have studied the happiness of anticipation and have found that the pleasure of looking forward to an event is often greater than the event itself. A 2010 study reported that planning a trip can make you happier than the actual journey. Vacationers experienced a boost in joy while researching the journey because they anticipated good times ahead.[5]

Because we have discovered that life here on earth will never satisfy, you might wonder if our current existence will always appear dark and dismal. No; we can still find joy. We can find joy in the unmet desire for the world beyond what we can see, and that is more gratifying than every other *satisfied* desire. One of the greatest sources of pleasure is in our anticipation of heaven, where all our longings will be met.

When I worship God, delight in Him, and focus on His faithfulness, I look forward to the joy I will have when I see Him face-to-face. The more I cling to His promises and trust that the final destination of my life will be more stupendous than I can imagine, the more my anticipation builds and the more joy I experience.

The writer of Hebrews talked about the heroes of faith like Abel, Abraham, and Sarah who lived in anticipation:

These all died in faith, not having received the things promised, but having seen them and greeted them from afar, and having acknowledged that they were strangers and exiles on the earth. For people who speak thus make it clear that they are seeking a homeland. If they had been thinking of that land from which they had gone out, they would have had opportunity to return. But as it is, they desire a better country, that is, a heavenly one. Therefore God is not ashamed to be called their God, for He has prepared for them a city. (Hebrews 11:13–16)

The great Old Testament heroes of faith trusted God even though they didn't see the fulfillment of the promise of a Messiah. Their examples can inspire us, reminding us that we are "strangers and exiles" on earth, suffering homesickness for a home we have not yet experienced but which we know God is preparing for us. We live in expectation of this homeland.

Like my experience in anticipating the hugs and heart-to-heart conversations that are impossible or difficult on Skype, we can look forward to the joy of seeing Jesus face-to-face and living a new existence without pain or heartache.

> When I give God my desires, they lose their grip on my soul.

Look Forward to Goodness

In addition to living in the joy of anticipation of a heavenly destination, we can look forward to the good gifts God has planned for us here on earth. One of my favorite verses in the Book of Psalms is Psalm 31:19:

> Oh, how abundant is Your goodness,
>   which You have stored up for those who fear You
> and worked for those who take refuge in You,
>   in the sight of the children of mankind!

When I read those words, I picture a closet with my name on the door. (Maybe even one designed by the Closet Experts?) Inside, God has many blessings stored up for me. Things I know nothing about now but trust to be amazing blessings He will give at the right time.

Rab, the Hebrew word translated here as "abundant," means "much, many, abounding"—enough. God has not set aside a tiny linen closet for me. The storage space with my name on it is a huge walk-in closet with multiple shelves and drawers and racks and rods. Inside, the Father has stashed many layers of goodness. He has stockpiled enough. My God is not a stingy God. Sometimes I forget that. When I look at what I don't have, I tend to think of God holding out on me. But His Word reminds me of His generosity.

What God has stored up for me is His goodness. In Psalm 31:19, the Hebrew word *tuwb* means "good things," "beauty," and "joy." Life on earth often gives us pain, loneliness, sickness, and broken relationships, but God wants to give us beauty and joy. *Tuwb* is also used in Exodus 33:18, where Moses asked God to show His glory. God told Moses that He would put Moses in a cleft in the rock and make all His *tuwb* pass by. God's true nature is goodness. Jesus reminded His followers, "If you then, who are evil, know how to give good gifts to your children, how much more will your Father who is in heaven give good things to those who ask Him!" (Matthew 7:11). God wants to give us good gifts.

However, not all of God's good gifts are in the currency of this world. God promises the good gifts of the Spirit, like love, joy, peace, patience, kindness, goodness, faithfulness (Galatians 5:22), given through Word and Sacrament. And according to Psalm 31:19, God has stored some of the blessings He has planned for us. The Hebrew word means "to hide, treasure, or store up." It's the same word used when Moses' mother hid him for three months (Exodus 2:2). Some of the things God has for us are behind the closet door, hidden from view. When things get tough, it helps me to picture that closet full of blessings God has set aside specifically for me. I can't see them now and may not see some of them until heaven, but I know they are there.

Living in anticipation of God's blessings helps me to live with enough for now. I remember God's true nature of goodness and that He has stored up what is best for me. If I focus on His kindness, I can trust He will open the storage closet and distribute the blessings at just the right time.

Prayer Prompt

Take a minute to read all of Psalm 31. Choose a few favorite verses and turn them into a prayer.

_____

_____

_____

_____

_____

_____

_____

_____

_____

Experience "Enough for Now" Moments

While part of living with "enough for now" means living in anticipation of the blessings God will give in the future, another facet is appreciating the gifts God has already given. I often struggle with this. I try to tell myself, _If God hasn't given me an item from His storage closet yet, it must mean I don't need it now._ But I would rather have the object of my desire in my actual closet where I can see it instead of trusting God for the future. Like the rich fool, I make happiness contingent on having a surplus for times to come.

But often God doesn't give a surplus because He wants us to depend on Him daily. We see this in the Lord's Prayer: "Give us this day our daily bread" (Matthew 6:11). "Daily bread" seems a foreign concept to me. Every week I drive to the grocery store, fill up my trunk with bags of food, and pull into my attached garage to unload enough provisions for a week. In addition, my freezer is jam-packed. My pantry has dozens of cans and jars of delicious things to eat. If I needed to, I could probably live on the food in my freezer and pantry for a month or more.

DAILY TRUSTING

I would always prefer that God would give me more than enough. I feel so much more secure when my cupboards are stocked and the bank account is full. But sometimes God doesn't give a surplus because He wants us to depend on Him daily.

We see this in the way He cared for the children of Israel in the wilderness. He provided manna for them every day. Each morning they gathered what they needed for their family. If they tried to store up extra for the next day, it turned rancid and became filled with maggots. The one exception was the sixth day when the people were also to gather enough for the Sabbath.

As our loving Father, God wants us to come to Him every day with our needs. He desires us to trust in His goodness—and not in our surplus.

But when we visit China, I see people who experience the "daily bread" concept. Most people live in apartments and take the bus to work. They stop at the grocery store on their way home from work and pick up what they need for dinner that night and breakfast the next day. They can't carry a week's worth of food on the bus or lug it up seven flights of stairs. (In China, buildings are not required to have elevators unless they have more than eight floors.) They buy enough for now.

We are "strangers and exiles" on earth, suffering homesickness for a home we have not yet experienced, but which we know God is preparing for us.

Like the Chinese people who visit the grocery store every day, God wants us to depend on Him daily for our needs. And we are not only to come to Him in petition but in thanksgiving. "As Christians, we pray that we might be grateful for everything (however ordinary) that God provides each day for our bodily life."[6] Instead of complaining about what we don't have, we are to appreciate what God has already given.

One way to do this is to look for "enough for now" moments in our lives. I admit I am not always good at this, but I can remember the first time I consciously thought, *I want to fully enjoy and remember this amazing moment.* I was nineteen and riding on a bus with seventeen other musicians on our way to perform in California. We were driving through the Sierra

Nevadas on a cloudless day. I wanted to memorize every detail: the brilliant blue sky, the pure white snow on the mountains, the scent of spring coming through the bus windows, and the sound of the laughter on the bus mixed with the Keith Green song playing on the speakers. It seemed life couldn't get any better than what I had in that moment.

Since then, I've experienced other "enough for now" moments—times when my heart was so full of gratitude that I didn't even think about what I didn't have. Moments like holding my newborn babies, hiking in Zion National Park with my husband, listening to the Chicago Symphony perform a Rachmaninoff piano concerto at Ravinia Park, praising God in a heart-stirring worship service. I've memorized these special times, but if I pay attention, every day has "enough for now" moments: my first sip of white peach oolong tea in the morning, my husband's hand in mine as we walk around the neighborhood, an email from a friend asking if I have time to go out to lunch, the sound of the rain against the window, and the song on the car radio reminding me I am never alone.

> My God is not a stingy God. . . . His Word reminds me of His generosity.

Experiencing "enough for now" means living in gratitude for God's daily care. When I quit trying to store up an abundance for the future and instead concentrate on the gifts God has given, my heart is full, my soul content.

Exercising Enough

Make a list of things you are grateful for right now. How does gratitude help you live with "enough for now"?

_____

_____

_____

_____

_____

_____

Live Unsatisfied

At the beginning of this chapter, I shared Augustine's words, "The whole life of the good Christian is a holy longing." C. S. Lewis once said that if we long for things that the world cannot satisfy, then that means we were made for another world.

It seems counterintuitive, but I have learned to live with "enough for now" by realizing I will never be completely satisfied on this earth. "Enough" simply isn't available on our planet.

As Christians, our souls yearn for God. Right now "we see in a mirror dimly" (1 Corinthians 13:12). We have only a glimpse of what heaven will be like. Yes, we experience many blessings of eternity right now: We enjoy the freedom from eternal punishment of our sins because of Jesus' sacrifice on the cross. We can hear God's words of unconditional love to us in Scripture. We receive comfort, strength, and encouragement from the Holy Spirit. But we long for the time when we will see God face-to-face.

Author Amy Simpson calls this "living unsatisfied." In her book *Blessed Are the Unsatisfied*, she proposes a difference between dissatisfaction and "unsatisfaction." She writes, "Dissatisfaction is an active—sometimes even purposeful—absence, rejection, or refusal of satisfaction in a context where satisfaction is expected. It breeds discontent, contempt, and a feeling of emptiness."[7]

> I have learned to live with "enough for now" by realizing that I will never be completely satisfied on this earth. "Enough" simply isn't available on our planet.

On the other hand, "unsatisfaction is something more like acceptance combined with anticipation. . . . It is a desire that can live with deferral, an embrace of the God-shaped vacuum in us and a commitment to stop trying to make it full, a healthy hunger that is content to wait for the feast."[8]

She likens it to waiting for Thanksgiving Day dinner. Your mouth is watering as your nose detects the aromas of the roasting turkey and the cinnamon-laden pumpkin pie. Dissatisfaction complains about having to wait for the turkey to cook and may even try to calm the hunger pains with junk food.

Unsatisfaction embraces the tummy rumblings, enjoys the smells of the upcoming feast, and waits.

Living unsatisfied speaks to the rumblings of our souls: "Something better than you can imagine is coming. Stop attempting to fill up on what the world offers because it simply won't 'hit the spot.' You will still crave more."

Living unsatisfied means not expecting the "appetizers" this world offers to fully sate our hunger. God's good gifts in this world give temporary pleasure, but they often increase our appetite for lasting joy. When we accept the fact that complete happiness is not available here, we avoid living in constant disappointment.

> Living unsatisfied means not expecting the "appetizers" this world offers to fully sate our hunger.

Living unsatisfied doesn't mean settling for less. It means fully expecting abundance from God—but with the willingness to wait. Dissatisfaction and discouragement because of what we now possess are replaced with the confidence that fulfillment is a sure thing—someday in God's perfect timing.

I have lived too long like the rich fool, constantly looking for happiness and contentment in having more. But as I delved into Jesus' parable and placed myself in the story, I learned I will never find enough here because enough doesn't exist on this planet. In the meantime, I can trust the God of sufficiency and ask Him to transform my desires. I can appreciate the gifts the Lord has given and live with a holy longing for what is to come.

And that is enough for now.

WHAT IS YOUR BIGGEST TAKEAWAY FROM THIS CHAPTER?

_____

_____

_____

_____

_____

O GOD OF SUFFICIENCY,

I praise You for Your boundless generosity in providing me with a way to know You and be with You for eternity. Forgive me when I have trivialized these lavish gifts and have looked for satisfaction in this broken world.

Your many earthly gifts can bring joy, but they can never fully satisfy my soul, for it is made for heaven. This truth frees my soul from the endless cycle of searching for fulfillment, only to obtain disappointment and disillusionment.

Help me to rejoice in the gifts You have already given and live in anticipation of a glorious future with You where all my longings will be met. Let me rest in Your provision and live with enough for now. In Jesus' name. Amen.

EPILOGUE

I closed the door behind me and walked into the night. Using a flashlight to guide my way in the pitch-black darkness, I picked my way over tree roots and stones. When I reached the lake, I walked out onto the dock and took a seat on the bench. I switched off my flashlight and looked up. This was the light show I had left the cozy cottage for.

Like a billion sequins on a black velvet dress, the stars sparkled and shone. A wide swath of sky we call the Milky Way looked like the sequin jar had simply tipped over—there were too many sparkles to count or even individually distinguish. Smooth as glass, the lake reflected the beauty of the sky. Quiet reigned. The stillness was only occasionally interrupted by the muted splash of a fish coming up to catch a bug or the plaintive call of a loon. I sat in the cool night air and drank in the beauty.

We were spending a week in the north woods of Wisconsin—"up north" as the locals say. I enjoyed these relaxed days of reading in the rented cottage, hiking in the woods, or exploring souvenir shops in town. I appreciated the quiet evenings of simple suppers and roasting marshmallows over the open fire (s'mores, anyone?). But the nights—I relished the magical nights. Every night the sky was clear, I left my family to their Scrabble games and Rummikub matches in the cottage and walked down to the lake, where I had a view of God's glory unobstructed by trees. A view that is impossible in light-polluted Chicagoland where I live. A view that drew my heart to my Creator.

The sight of a million stars reminded me of the enormity of my Maker. The sky silently shouted the Lord's glory and majesty. I sensed my smallness—but also my value. Though I am only a minuscule part of God's creation, I know that He loves me, sacrificed His Son for me, and puts on magnificent light shows for me.

During the day, I had a limited view of the universe. I became focused on my life in the here and now: my successes, my failures, my problems, my complaints. But at night, when God drew back the curtain, I was reminded of the enormity of His creation and of how much more waits for me in eternity.

I knew we would soon leave the cottage in the North Woods and drive back to our chaotic lives in Chicago. There, we'd struggle to pay the bills and grapple with our too-busy schedules. Arguments over silly issues would mar our relationships. I would simultaneously grumble about folding our numerous laundered clothes and complain I had nothing to wear. Mint chocolate chip ice cream would scream my name, and the next day I would step onto the scale and wish I hadn't given in to the craving. Contentment would stay just out of reach.

Life isn't perfect. But for the moment—this tiny sliver of time when I felt overcome by both God's magnificence and His care for me, His insignificant daughter—it was enough.

We are at the end of our journey to "enough," and what we have discovered is that all of our longings are shadows of heaven. Perhaps that is why I am drawn to the glitter of the stars and the iridescent Milky Way. When I see them, I remember that there is so much more than this world. I cannot see it now, cannot even fathom it, but the stars whisper the reality of heaven.

In this life, we will continue to strive for enough. Bills loom large, and we may lack sufficient money to pay them. The stuff in our closets and cupboards will at times seem like too much and at others not enough. We struggle with the issue of enough food. Our relationships may not satisfy us. We never have adequate time to do the things we must do, let alone the activities we want to do. The world constantly tells us we are not attractive enough, smart enough, or successful enough.

The rich fool in Jesus' parable did not experience enough. Even though he clearly owned a sufficient amount to meet his needs, he told his soul happiness would come when he had more. Like many of us, he equated more stuff with more satisfaction.

But Jesus taught that the storing up of goods, money, or influence will never satisfy. He warned His followers to guard against greed—the constant quest for more. The journey of more does not lead to satisfaction.

The only way I can find contentment in this life is to rest in the God of sufficiency.

To trust that He is more than able to meet all my needs.

To release my wishes into His hands and allow Him to recalibrate my desires.

To live "unsatisfied" right now and live in anticipation of all the goodness God the Son has prepared for me in the future.

To gratefully pay attention to God's daily blessings.

Then I will have enough for now—in Christ.

STUDY GUIDE

Go further on your journey to "enough" by delving into the pages of Scripture. The study questions that follow will help you discover how God leads us to find "enough for now," even in this broken and disappointing world. I have organized the questions in levels—not levels of difficulty, but levels of time.

LEVEL 1: Reflect on the Reading. If you have only fifteen minutes, complete this section. These questions will help you reflect on the chapter's lessons and make them more personal. If you are doing the study in a group, these questions will also start conversation flowing.

LEVEL 2: Dig into Scripture. If you have more time, dive deeper into the Word by doing a verse -mapping exercise. The process is explained in the study questions for chapter 1. It may look daunting, but it only takes ten to twelve minutes, especially if you use online tools.

LEVEL 3: Apply the Word to Your Life. At this level, you will discover how the principles of contentment and finding enough can be used in your ordinary days.

LEVEL 4: Cultivate Enough. These activities will help you internalize what you learned. You will experience the knowledge in new ways through practical exercises, art, music, and hands-on activities.

To get the most out of this study, I encourage you to complete all the levels. But life is hectic—do what you can!

May the activities in this study guide lead you closer to the God of sufficiency—the only source of "enough."

The Author

CHAPTER 1   **WHAT IS ENOUGH?** STUDY QUESTIONS

Reflect on the Reading

1. If a local charity called you today and asked if you had any clothing or small household goods to donate, how would you respond?

yes! Where can I drop them off.

2. Look up the word *enough* in a thesaurus. Take note of some of the synonyms. Use some of these synonyms to write your own definition of *enough*.

Enough is not only adequate or sufficient, in my life it is greatly abundant.

3. Place an *X* on the line below to indicate your general satisfaction with your life.

_____   I don't have enough.
_____   I have enough.
___X___   I have too much.

Why did you place the *X* there?

I'm trying to pare down my possessions to simplify my life to what is important.

Dig into Scripture

In each chapter of this book, you will dig deeper into God's Word through verse mapping. This method of Bible study researches everything about a verse to learn more about God and what He wants for you. It helps you to take the verse apart, examine each element, and then put it back together with a greater understanding. We will research context, translations, cross-references, and word meanings. Here's how:

WRITE:

Write out the verse from your favorite translation. Highlight the most important words.

CONTEXT:

Look at what is happening in Scripture before and after this verse.

TRANSLATIONS:

Look up this verse in other translations/versions of the Bible. An easy tool to use for this is **BibleGateway.com**. You can also use a parallel Bible or the other versions you have on your shelf.

CROSS-REFERENCES:

If you have a study Bible, it will include cross-references—a list of verses related to the one you are studying. You can also use an online Bible for this.

WORD MEANINGS:

Next, take a closer look at the words you originally highlighted when you first wrote out the verse. Find each word in a dictionary and write out the meaning. If you want to find out the meaning of the word in the language in which it was originally written in, you can use **BlueLetterBible.com**. Type in the verse, then click "Tools" beside the verse. The interlinear Bible will show you each word along with the original Greek or Hebrew word. Click on the Strong's number and it will give you the meaning of the word. Write out the meanings that apply to the verse you are studying.

PARAPHRASE:

Now that you have dissected the verse, put it back together. Using what you have learned through other translations, context, cross-references, and word study, write out the verse in your own words. Remember, we are not rewriting the Bible but internalizing the meaning by writing a paraphrase faithful to the holy authors.

On the next two pages, I have done a verse map of 1 Timothy 6:6–7. Then it's your turn to try it with Luke 12:32.

VERSE MAPPING: **1 TIMOTHY 6:6–7**

Write out the verse from your favorite translation of the Bible. Highlight important words.

> But godliness with contentment is great gain, for we brought nothing into the world, and we cannot take anything out of the world.

Context: What is happening before and after this verse?

> Before this, Paul warns against false teachers that speak against the teachings of Jesus and do not teach in accord with godliness. After this verse, Paul advises fleeing from temptations of money and riches, and pursuing righteousness, godliness, and faith.

Other versions: Look up 1 Timothy 6:6–7 in different translations. Write out your favorites here.

> But godliness actually is a means of great gain when accompanied by contentment. For we have brought nothing into the world, so we cannot take anything out of it either. (NASB)

> Now godliness with contentment is great gain. For we brought nothing into this world, and it is certain we can carry nothing out. (NKJV)

Cross-references: What other Scripture passages are related to this verse?

> For while bodily training is of some value, godliness is of value in every way, as it holds promise for the present life and also for the life to come. (1 Timothy 4:8)

> Better is the little that the righteous has than the abundance of many wicked. (Psalm 37:16)

Choose some of the words you highlighted in 1 Timothy 6:6–7. Write
them here, then look them up in a Greek and/or English dictionary.

> godliness

Greek *eusebeia*: reverence, respect, piety toward God;
English: *godly*—conforming to the laws and wishes of God

> contentment

Greek *autarkeia*: sufficiency, a mind contented with its lot;
English: a state of satisfaction

> gain

Greek *porismos*: to acquire or procure for oneself;
English: to get something desired

> world

Greek *kosmos*: an orderly arrangement, world, universe,
the world with all its people and cultures; English: the earth

Paraphrase: Write out the verse in your own words, using what you have
learned.

> Beware of greed! Godliness—living in reverence to God by
> conforming to His laws—is actually great wealth if we live in
> a state of satisfaction, content with what God has given us. I
> need to remember that when I was born into this world, I had
> nothing, and when I die, I cannot take any of my possessions
> with me.

Now it's your turn.

VERSE MAPPING: **LUKE 12:32**

Write out the verse from your favorite translation of the Bible. Highlight
important words.

> Fear not, little flock, for it is your
> Father's good pleasure to give you the
> Kingdom. Sell your possessions, and
> give to the needy. Provide

Context: What is happening before and after this verse?

Parable of rich fool, do not be
anxious, God takes care of all
creatures.
Be prepared for the return of the
Son of Man.

Other versions: Look up Luke 12:32 in different translations. Write out
your favorites here.

all very similar - Like the Lutheran
Study Bible

John 10:10

Cross-references: What other Scripture passages are related to this verse?

John 10:10

Choose some of the words you highlighted in Luke 12:32. Write them
here, then look them up in a Greek and/or English dictionary.

Fear not

good pleasure

give you -

Paraphrase: Write out the verse in your own words, using what you have
learned. Don't be afraid, my family your
Father is resolved to give you the
Kingdom. delights

Apply the Word to Your Life

1. Read Luke 12:13–21.

    a. State the lesson of the parable of the rich fool in your own words.

    You can't take it with you. Share your wealth with others.

    b. How are you like the rich man? How are you different? *In some aspect we're all like the rich man. We all like the comforts of life + the "security" of having worldly riches.*
    false

    c. When does the rich man think he will be happy (or merry) (vv. 18–19)?

    When he has "ample goods" which he will never reach.

    d. How would you define *enough* in your life?

2. Read Luke 12:22–34.

    a. Write the lesson of Jesus' teaching in your own words.

    The Kingdom of God takes priority over possessions. God will take care of us.

    b. According to this passage, how do we normally react to not having enough food or clothing (v. 22)? How does this relate to the rich man's reaction in the parable? *Anxiety! Having more will relieve his anxiety.*

    c. Why is this reaction unnecessary (vv. 30–32)?

    God will provide.

    d. Can you think of a period in your life when you felt satisfied—when you thought, *Now I have enough?* Describe what life looked like in that moment. How were you able to say those words?

    most of the time. — job losses

    e. Now describe a time in your life when you definitely did not have enough. What was happening? How did you cope? How did God come through?

    Job loss — after building new house

Cultivate Enough

1. The rich man cultivated his fields and had an oversupply of food but not an abundance of contentment. How can we cultivate a sense of enough? Let's start by examining our desires. Set aside 15–30 minutes. Begin by reflecting on Luke 12:13–34. Then consider: In what areas of life do you feel you do not have enough? Ask yourself questions like these: What stirs up anxiety in your heart? What do you think of first in the morning? What keeps you tossing and turning at night? What does a friend have that you wish you had? When you have some free time, what do you think about?

Money to travel + give away

Write some of your desires, using these categories as prompts:

Money _____

Stuff _____

Food _____

Relationships _____

Time _____

Self-Image _____

Now focus on one of these desires. Bravely lay it on the altar. Surrender it to our loving Father. Tell Him you trust Him to do the right thing with it—to fulfill the longing or to say no and give you something better. Ask Him to help you understand His timing and appreciate the way He increases your patience and faith as you await His best. Use the space here to write your prayer, if you wish.

2. Create an artistic rendering of our memory verse: "Fear not, little flock, for it is your Father's good pleasure to give you the kingdom" (Luke 12:32). Use your drawing talents or your computer's many fonts to produce a reminder of God's "enoughness" for us. Tuck your creation into your Bible or post it on your refrigerator.

3. Worship the God of sufficiency with the words of a hymn or song. Look up the hymn "Great Is Thy Faithfulness" (LSB 809) or find the song "Enough" by Chris Tomlin on YouTube.

CHAPTER 2 **ENOUGH MONEY** STUDY QUESTIONS

Reflect on the Reading

1. Write about a time in your life when you struggled with a lack of money. If this struggle was in the past, how do you now see God working during that difficult period? If this is a current struggle, how are you focusing on the God of enough during this hard time?

2. Write your reaction to this statement: Much of our problem with enough in the area of money comes from comparing ourselves with the wrong group of people.

3. Place an *X* on the line below to indicate your satisfaction with your current finances.

_____ I don't have enough money.

_____ I have enough money.

_____ I have too much money.

Why did you place the *X* there? (Or did you just laugh at the last statement?)

Dig into Scripture

Use the verse-mapping technique to dig into Luke 12:33–34. Look back at pages 148–49 for instructions on this Bible study method.

VERSE MAPPING: **LUKE 12:33–34**

Write out the verses from your favorite translation of the Bible. Highlight important words.

Context: What is happening before and after these verses?

Other versions: Look up Luke 12:33–34 in different translations. Write out your favorites here.

Cross-references: What other Scripture passages are related to these verses?

Choose some of the words you highlighted in Luke 12:33–34. Write them here, then look them up in a Greek and/or English dictionary.

Paraphrase: Write out the verses in your own words, using what you have learned.

Apply the Word to Your Life

1. Reread the parable of the rich fool, Luke 12:16–21.

    a. How did the rich fool demonstrate that he based his security on wealth?

    b. How did he show his wealth was a source of his feelings of importance?

    c. How can you see he did not understand the concept of true riches?

    d. Let's take an honest self-check. Rate yourself from 1 to 5 in each of the following areas, 1 meaning that you strongly disagree with the statement and 5 meaning that you strongly agree with the statement.

I often base my sense of security on money.	1	2	3	4	5
Money and material wealth are a significant basis of my self-esteem.	1	2	3	4	5
I hate to admit it, but I find myself spending more time and energy on accumulating the things of earth instead of the things of heaven.	1	2	3	4	5

e. Which area got the highest score? What have you learned from our study on money that can help you in this area?

2. Read 1 Timothy 6:6–10 and 17–19.

a. What ideas or phrases jump out at you from this passage?

b. Paul talks about "godliness with contentment" (v. 6), which I see as the direct opposite of the *pleonexia* we saw in the rich fool. Describe what godliness with contentment might look like in the twenty-first century.

c. What in this passage can help when the world tempts us to base our security in money?

d. What in Paul's words can prevent us from centering our self-worth on our net worth?

e. How does Paul advise avoiding the temptation of accumulating more and more material wealth?

Cultivate Enough

1. Jesus said, "Where your treasure is, there your heart will be also" (Matthew 6:21). In modern terms, He is saying, "Look at your checkbook, your credit card statements, your receipts and you will discover what your priorities are. You will find what your heart gravitates toward."

Take a look at your checkbook and credit card statements and write some of the categories where your money goes (e.g., housing, food, medical expenses, clothes, technology, entertainment). What does this tell you about your heart?

2. The rich fool in Jesus' parable thought he had enough for the good life because he built bigger barns and stored up more of his goods. Living in our materialistic society, we are often tempted to follow his example. The world tells us we need more money to have more security and to experience more happiness. Deep down we know this isn't true. As children of God, we have a loving heavenly Father—the true Provider of the good life.

When Satan and our culture tempt us to find our "enough" in money, let's turn to the God of sufficiency and read His promises of provision.

Look up some of these verses and briefly tell how God provides.

Genesis 22:14_____

Psalm 23:1_____

Matthew 7:11 _____

Romans 8:32 _____

Philippians 4:19_____

Choose your favorite verse and post it where you will see it often in the coming days. Remind yourself of the God of "enough." If you wish, create a poster of this verse using your art supplies or computer. Or illustrate the verse in the margins of your Bible.

3. Worship the God of sufficiency with the words of the hymn "All Depends on Our Possessing" (*LSB* 732) or the worship song "Forever Reign" by Hillsong.

CHAPTER 3 **ENOUGH STUFF** STUDY QUESTIONS

Reflect on the Reading

1. Have you ever felt overwhelmed by your stuff? How? When?

Whenever I move.

2. Describe your reaction to this statement: Satan knows that the more he keeps us busy buying, cleaning, organizing, dusting, filing, washing, arranging, displaying, polishing, tuning, vacuuming, repairing, painting, and maintaining our possessions, the less time we will have for our relationship with God.

True — although it does keeps us out of worse trouble.

3. Place an **X** on the line below to indicate your satisfaction with your current level of possessions.

_____ I don't have enough stuff.

_**X**_ I have enough stuff.

_↓_ I have too much stuff.

Why did you put the **X** there?

Am trying to get rid of more

Dig into Scripture

Use the verse-mapping technique to dig into Luke 12:15. Look back at pages 148–49 for instructions on this Bible study method.

VERSE MAPPING: **LUKE 12:15**

Write out the verse from your favorite translation of the Bible. Highlight important words.

Take care, and be on guard against all covetousness for one's life does not consist in the abundance of his possessions

Context: What is happening before and after this verse?

Jesus is asked to arbitrate between 2 brothers regarding dividing an inheritance

Other versions: Look up Luke 12:15 in different translations. Write out your favorites here. *Living Bible — Paraphrased*

Cross-references: What other Scripture passages are related to this verse?

I Tim 6:6-10 Love of money the root of all evil
Matt: 4-4

Choose some of the words you highlighted in Luke 12:15. Write them here, then look them up in a Greek and/or English dictionary.

Covetousness — Merriam-Webster · eager or excessive desire esp. for wealth or possession

Paraphrase: Write out the verse in your own words, using what you have learned. *Be content with what you have*

Apply the Word to Your Life

1. The rich fool talked about *his* crops, *his* barns, *his* grain, *his* goods.

   a. What do these verses have to say about ownership?

      Deuteronomy 10:14 *Ten Commandments*

      1 Chronicles 29:11–12 *all that is in heaven + earth is Gods.*

      Psalm 50:10–12 *all is Gods'*

   b. In view of these Scripture passages, I encourage you to write a "transfer of title" to the Lord, acknowledging Him as the owner of all your stuff. Sign it, date it, and post it in a prominent place to remind you that "your" stuff is not your own but God's.

   Suggestion:

   I now recognize God as the true owner of all "my" money and possessions. From this day on, I will prayerfully ask Him how He wants me to use all of the things He has given me to use.

   Signed _____ Date _____

2. Read Jonah 2:7–9.

   a. How do we sometimes treat our things more like idols than ordinary possessions? *They become the centre of our life - our life revolves around them.*

b. How can these idols cause us to "forsake [our] hope of steadfast love" (v. 8)?

They replace God – God takes a back seat to our personal desires.

c. Why is thanksgiving sometimes a sacrifice (v. 9)?

d. How can giving thanks to God change us?

It changes the focus from us and our possessions to God + thankfulness.

3. Read Luke 14:12–24.

   a. Many people were invited to the banquet. What excuses did they offer for not attending?

   1. Bought a field - must go see it.
   2 "   "   " yoke of oxen - must examine them
   3. married a wife

   b. In Scripture, a banquet is often an image for the kingdom of God. How do we in the modern world sometimes act like the people in the parable, offering excuses to God's invitation?

   c. Who ultimately attended the banquet? What lesson might you glean from this?

   Poor, crippled, blind and lame.

Cultivate Enough

Try one of these projects:

1. Take a weeklong spending fast. During the next seven days, purchase nothing new (except necessities like food, medicine, and gasoline). Enjoy what you already own. Wear the clothes in your closet, eat the food in your refrigerator, read the books on your shelves.

   What did you learn from this experience? Journal your thoughts.

2. Every day this week, get rid of one item. To make this exercise easier, designate a box where you will put the discarded things. At the end of the week, take the box to a charity that could use those items. (To boost the challenge, you might decide to get rid of two or five or ten things each day!)

   How did this exercise change your closets and other storage spaces? How did it affect your attitude toward stuff?

3. Grab a piece of paper and write down everything you own. Okay, that might be too overwhelming. Start with one room or one drawer. Count how many things you have. For most of us, it won't take long to realize how very much we already have.

Take the list of things in your room or drawer and say a prayer of thanks for each item. Did this exercise change your perspective? How?

4. Take a few minutes to worship the God of sufficiency. Some ideas for a song include "This Is Our God" by Hillsong, "Always Enough" by Kari Jobe, and "God of Grace and God of Glory" (*LSB* 850).

CHAPTER 4   **ENOUGH FOOD** STUDY QUESTIONS

Reflect on the Reading

1. What food is your biggest temptation?

 *Chocolate*

2. Contemplate this question: What if our cravings for enough food are meant to draw us to Jesus, the bread of life? How might your day be different if your food cravings led you to Jesus?

3. Circle the phrases below that describe your relationship with food.

　　※ I tend to eat healthy most of the time.　　I go to food for comfort.

　　　　I'm always thinking about food.　　I try to avoid food.

　The temptation of food is my biggest downfall.　　I can never get enough food.

　　I struggle with making healthy food choices.　　Chocolate is my friend. ※

4. What changes would you like to make after reading this chapter on food?

Dig into Scripture

Use the verse-mapping technique to dig into Luke 12:29. Look back at pages 148–49 for instructions on this Bible study method.

VERSE MAPPING: **LUKE 12:29**

Write out this verse from your favorite translation of the Bible. Highlight
important words.

Context: What is happening before and after this verse?

Clothes

Seek his kingdom

Other versions: Look up Luke 12:29 in different translations. Write out your
favorites here.

Cross-references: What other Scripture passages are related to this verse?

James 1: 6

Choose some of the words you highlighted in Luke 12:29. Write them here,
then look them up in a Greek and/or English dictionary.

"lack of trust in God.

Paraphrase: Write out the verse in your own words, using what you have learned.

Apply the Word to Your Life

1. Food is often the place we go when we're stressed and anxious. This week pay attention to your eating habits. When you're tempted to turn to food for reasons other than hunger, ask yourself these questions:
   - What's happening right now that is making me want to eat?
   - What am I feeling?
   - How will this food help my emotions?

Then remember Jesus' words "Life is more than food" (Luke 12:23), and ask yourself one more question:

   - How does God want me to respond to my current emotions?

Write some of your experiences in this journaling space or use the chart on the next page.

FOOD TEMPTATION (What kind of food was I craving?)	EMOTION (What was I feeling?)	RESPONSE (What did I do?)

2. Jesus said, "Blessed are those who hunger and thirst for righteousness, for they shall be satisfied" (Matthew 5:6). Instead of craving pepperoni pizza and hot fudge sundaes, we are to crave righteousness. Let's explore this concept of righteousness.

   a. Look up the following verses and write what you discover about righteousness.

   Psalm 71:19

   Proverbs 21:21

Romans 3:21–22

Romans 4:5

Ephesians 6:14

b. *Righteousness* is defined as "the state of him who is as he ought to be, righteousness, the condition acceptable to God."[1] Using what you've learned from this definition and from the Scriptures you read, answer these questions:
Practically speaking, what does it look like to hunger and thirst after righteousness?

How can a yearning for righteousness curb my unhealthy cravings?

3. When Jesus was tempted with food, He used the weapon of God's Word to fight Satan. Let's do the same. Reread the Scripture passages on page 73. Then write out the following verses. Circle the ones most meaningful to you.
Psalm 34:8

Psalm 90:14

Luke 1:53

Luke 12:22–23

John 6:35

Write out your favorite verses and post them on your refrigerator, cupboard, or pantry door. Whenever you have an unhealthy craving, try filling yourself with God's Word first.

Cultivate Enough

1. This week, consider fasting from the food you wrote down in answer to the first question in "Reflect on the Reading"—the one food most difficult for you to resist. Use your craving for this food to draw you to Jesus, the bread of life. You may need to plan ahead to be successful in this limited fast.

How can you change your physical environment to help you resist this food (e.g., purge the house of the contraband; lock the cupboard where it is stored)?

How will you need to change your routine to avoid this food (e.g., take a different route to work that doesn't go past the doughnut shop; avoid watching TV in the evenings)?

What healthier food options could replace this food (e.g., Greek yogurt and fruit instead of ice cream; air-popped popcorn instead of chips)?

What will you do when a craving comes (e.g., write a prayer in your journal asking God for His help; pull out your Scripture cards; remember that you can only satisfy your soul's cravings in God)?

What will you do if you fail (e.g., don't beat yourself up but realize your humanness and inability to be perfect; ask the Father for strength to resist temptation; admit your failing and receive God's grace)?

You might want to copy one of these mini-posters to hang in a prominent place this week.

ALL OF OUR
CRAVINGS
ARE MEANT
TO LEAD US
TO GOD.

YOUR BODY IS
A TEMPLE OF
THE HOLY SPIRIT
WITHIN YOU.
(1 Corinthians 6:19)

GENUINE,
MEANINGFUL LIFE
REQUIRES THE
NOURISHMENT OF
GOD'S HOLY WORD.

JESUS IS THE
BREAD OF LIFE—
THE ONE THING
THAT CAN SATISFY
ALL MY CRAVINGS.

AND DO NOT SEEK
WHAT YOU ARE
TO EAT AND WHAT
YOU ARE TO DRINK,
NOR BE WORRIED.
. . . INSTEAD, SEEK
HIS KINGDOM, AND
THESE THINGS WILL
BE ADDED TO YOU.
(Luke 12:29, 31)

2. Take a field trip this week to visit a food source. Depending on where you live and the time of year, you might visit an apple orchard, a pumpkin patch, or a field of strawberries. If those aren't possible, try a farmers market or simply your local grocery store. Wander around, taking in the sights and smells, and thank God for His generous and creative gifts of nourishment.

3. Worship with songs that talk of our hunger and thirst for God, like "As the Deer" by Martin Nystrom, "Hungry (Falling on My Knees)" by Kathryn Scott, or the hymns "Lord Jesus Christ, Life-Giving Bread" (*LSB* 625) and "Lord Jesus Christ, You Have Prepared" (*LSB* 622).

CHAPTER 5 **ENOUGH RELATIONSHIPS** STUDY QUESTIONS

Reflect on the Reading

1. Reread the box "People Who Need People" on page 78. Name some ways relationships have positively influenced your life.

Long friendships - confidence, that they have and will be with me no matter what.

2. Write your reaction to this statement: Greed and selfishness are major contributors to our broken relationships. Then consider: How have you been impacted by greed in your relationships with others? *G + S, - all about me, Marlene - never the same.*

3. Take an inventory of the relationships in your life. In the first column, list the relationships you have that build you up (e.g., family members and friends). In the second column, list those that you feel are missing or broken (e.g., you hope for a child; your relationship with your brother is damaged).

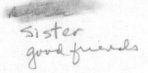

Sister
good friends

Relationships that build me up	Relationships that are missing or broken

Looking at the two sides, do you feel you have a deficit in relationships?

No.

Dig into Scripture

Use the verse-mapping technique to dig into 1 John 4:7. Look back at pages 148–49 for instructions on this Bible study method.

VERSE MAPPING: **1 JOHN 4:7**

Write out the verse from your favorite translation of the Bible. Highlight important words.

Context: What is happening before and after this verse?

The Spirit of Truth and the Spirit of Error - do are they from the world from God

If God loved us we should love each other.

Other versions: Look up 1 John 4:7 in different translations. Write out your
favorites here.

Lutheran study Bible

Cross-references: What other Scripture passages are related to this verse?

1 John Ch. 3. 11

Choose some of the words you highlighted in 1 John 4:7. Write them here,
then look them up in a Greek and/or English dictionary.

Love one another.
Love is from God.
Whoever loves has been born of God

God is love

Paraphrase: Write out the verse in your own words, using what you have learned.

God is Love and gives his love
to us that we love one another

Apply the Word to Your Life

1. Read Luke 12:13–15.

   a. What did the rich man want Jesus to do for him?

   Tell his brother to share his
   inheritance.

b. Why do you think Jesus declined? *It was an "earthly" issue — an earthly inheritance — Jesus was offering him a heavenly inheritance*

c. How have you seen greed negatively affect relationships? *relatives no longer talking to each other.*

d. Write a prayer asking God to show you where you have been the greedy one in your relationships. Ask Him to help you follow Christ's selfless giving.

2. Read Ecclesiastes 4:7–12.

a. What lesson do you take away from this passage?

Be joyful & do good as long as you live.

b. How do we sometimes prioritize material things over relationships?

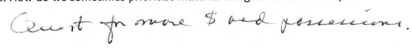
Quest for more $ and possessions.

c. Think of one way you could put the people in your life first this week (e.g., leave work early one day to take your child to the park after school; make time to call that friend who is hurting).

3. The relationships we have are beautiful gifts from God. But flawed humans will never completely satisfy our need for community. God is the only one who can be enough. Look up the following verses and write how God is enough in our relationships.

Passage	How God Is Enough
a. Psalm 6:9	He hears us and takes care of us.
b. Isaiah 54:5	The God of the whole earth.
c. John 15:15	Jesus calls us friends — not servants. He chose you + made all things known to us.
d. 1 Corinthians 8:3	If anyone loves God he is known by God.
e. Ephesians 1:4	We are predestined to be sons thru Jesus. We have redemption, forgiveness, + grace.
f. 1 John 3:1	He loved us so much that he made us his children.

Which of these is most meaningful to you right now? Write a prayer thanking God for being enough.

Cultivate Enough

1. Sing "What a Friend We Have in Jesus" (*LSB* 770) and thank God for the wonderful blessing of a close relationship with the Savior. Then substitute the word *are* for *have* and sing it again, thinking of how Jesus' love enables us to love and care for others. What can you learn from this hymn about how we do relationships when we rely on Christ?

   Jesus loves us no matter what — we can never match his love for us. An example to follow in our relationships with others,

2. This week, celebrate the relationships God has given you. Call a friend and set a lunch date. Or invite extended family members or friends to share a meal at your house. Make it potluck! Concentrate on the connections instead of the preparations.

3. When we find our "enough" in God and are filled with His love, we can then love the people God has placed in our lives. Take some time this week to let God "refill your pitcher." On these two pages, you will find verses that tell of God's love for us. Make a copy of the page and cut out the verses, placing them in prominent places or carrying them with you. Several times a day, spend a couple of minutes reading and contemplating one of the verses. You might even set an alarm to remind you to do this every hour or two. At the end of the day, record how this practice changed you and your relationships.

> For I am sure that neither death nor life,
> nor angels nor rulers, nor things present
> nor things to come, nor powers, nor height
> nor depth, nor anything else in all creation,
> will be able to separate us from the love
> of God in Christ Jesus our Lord.
> (Romans 8:38–39)

As the Father has loved Me, so have I loved you. Abide in My love. (John 15:9)

The LORD your God is in your midst, a mighty one who will save; He will rejoice over you with gladness; He will quiet you by His love; He will exult over you with loud singing. (Zephaniah 3:17)

Keep yourselves in the love of God, waiting for the mercy of our Lord Jesus Christ that leads to eternal life. (Jude 21)

Let Your steadfast love, O LORD, be upon us, even as we hope in You. (Psalm 33:22)

Satisfy us in the morning with Your steadfast love, that we may rejoice and be glad all our days. (Isaiah 54:10)

I have loved you with an everlasting love; therefore I have continued My faithfulness to you. (Jeremiah 31:3)

That you, being rooted and grounded in love, may have strength to comprehend with all the saints what is the breadth and length and height and depth, and to know the love of Christ that surpasses knowledge, that you may be filled with all the fullness of God. (Ephesians 3:17–19)

CHAPTER 6 **ENOUGH TIME** STUDY QUESTIONS

Reflect on the Reading

1. What would you do if you found out you could buy boxes of time at the dollar store?

2. What is your reaction to the story of "The Magic Thread"? How are you like Peter? How are you different?

3. How do you view time? Check all that apply.

_____A gift

_____ An opponent

_____ A scarce commodity

_____ A precious currency

_____ Something I need to control

Why did you check those options?

Dig into Scripture

Use the verse-mapping technique to dig into Luke 12:25–26. Look back at pages 148–49 for instructions on this Bible study method.

VERSE MAPPING: **LUKE 12:25–26**

Write out the verse from your favorite translation of the Bible. Highlight
important words.

Context: What is happening before and after this verse?

Other versions: Look up Luke 12:25–26 in different translations. Write out your
favorites here.

Cross-references: What other Scripture passages are related to this verse?

Luke 2:52
Matt 6:27

Choose some of the words you highlighted in Luke 12:25–26. Write them
here, then look them up in a Greek and/or English dictionary.

anxious

Paraphrase: Write out the verse in your own words, using what you have
learned.

Apply the Word to Your Life

1. One of the ways we can learn to use time well is to live with an eternity mind-set.

    a. What do the following verses tell you about our eternal God and the concept of forever?

    Job 36:26

God is

    Isaiah 51:6

    2 Peter 3:8

    Revelation 1:8

    b. Read Psalm 39:4–5.

    How does this psalm describe our lifetimes?

    Reflecting on this verse and on the illustration of 1 inch for a human lifetime versus 277 yards for an inadequate approximation of eternity, how does this change your view of time? Are there any changes you will make based on having an eternity mind-set?

c. What are some practical ways you can live with an eternity mind-set? Could you pray regularly for those you know and love who don't yet know Jesus? plan an event to invite neighbors to get to know them and plant seeds of the Gospel? ask God to direct your decisions about time? What are other ideas?

3. Read Luke 12:25 and Matthew 6:34.

a. In both passages, Jesus encourages us *not* to do something. What is that?

b. Name some ways anxiety about the future can rob us of joy in the present.

c. Read 1 Peter 1:6–9. According to this passage, what can we do *now*—even when we are tempted to worry about the future?

4. In the reading, we learned about *kairos* time. Read the following passages and write what you learn about *kairos*. (The words translated from the word *kairos* are italicized.)

a. Matthew 21:34: "When the *season* for fruit drew near, he sent his servants to the tenants to get his fruit."

b. Matthew 24:45: "Who then is the faithful and wise servant, whom his master has set over his household, to give them their food at the *proper time?*"

c. Acts 3:19–20: "Repent therefore, and turn back, that your sins may be blotted out, that *times* of refreshing may come from the presence of the Lord, and that He may send the Christ appointed for you, Jesus."

d. Galatians 6:10: "So then, as we have *opportunity*, let us do good to everyone, and especially to those who are of the household of faith."

How does the distinction between *chronos*, a quantity of time, and *kairos*, the quality of time, help you in your search for enough time?

Cultivate Enough

1. Do a schedule makeover.

   "Dump out" the contents of your calendar. Write down every one of your time commitments and responsibilities.

   Determine your essentials. List the activities you *must* do. Work, school, sleeping, and eating are all non-negotiable. Also include activities like exercising, meals with family, and worship. Block out time on your calendar for all these commitments. Determine how much time is left each week.

   Inventory your optional activities. List everything you and your family do that isn't on the essential list. Record things like PTA meetings, social activities, clubs and associations you belong to. List your kids' swimming lessons, chess club, and church activities. Estimate how much time each activity requires.

   Pray. Take each item on the optional list and pray about it. Ask God to give you the wisdom necessary to decide which items are worth your precious time. Ask yourself questions like these:

   - Does this activity benefit me and/or my neighbors for eternity?
   - Is this the right season of life for this activity?
   - Does this activity fit in with what I feel God is calling me to do?
   - Have I said yes to something that is *good* but not God's *best* for me right now?
   - Where can I do less?

   Decide what to cut and what to add. After praying about each activity, decide which ones deserve a place on your calendar and which ones need to be cut—either temporarily or permanently. Are there any pursuits you need to add?

   Put remaining activities into your schedule. Make sure the total responsibilities you commit to actually fit in the time available in your schedule without compromising the essentials. Don't forget to leave some margin—empty space on your calendar to accommodate emergencies and be available to help friends and family in need.

2. Set aside some *kairos* time for the purpose of spending it with Jesus. If possible, go to a park or your church sanctuary where you can worship without distractions. Take along your Bible and a notebook to read, listen, and record what God says to you during this quiet time.

3. Worship the God of sufficiency with song. Some ideas: "Abide with Me" (*LSB* 878) or "God of Our Yesterdays" by Matt Redman.

CHAPTER 7   **ENOUGH OF ME** STUDY QUESTIONS

Reflect on the Reading

1. Talk about a time when you felt you were not enough.

2. Try the three movies exercise I did at a writing conference.

a. Name three favorite movies.

Annie Hall
Fargo
West Side Story

b. Find a connecting theme.

Love, comedy
Fargo

c. How does this theme reflect your life passion?

3. Put an *X* on the line that best describes your personal feelings of enough (pretty enough, smart enough, talented enough, and so on).

I rarely feel I am enough.   I usually feel I am enough.

What are some factors that go into how you feel about yourself?

Dig into Scripture

Use the verse-mapping technique to dig into Luke 12:24. Look back at pages 148–49 for instructions on this Bible study method.

VERSE MAPPING: **LUKE 12:24**

Write out the verse from your favorite translation of the Bible. Highlight
important words.

Context: What is happening before and after this verse?

Other versions: Look up Luke 12:24 in different translations. Write out your
favorites here.

Cross-references: What other Scripture passages are related to this verse?

Choose some of the words you highlighted in Luke 12:24. Write them here,
then look them up in a Greek and/or English dictionary.

Paraphrase: Write out the verse in your own words, using what you have
learned.

Apply the Word to Your Life

1. Read Mark 9:33–37.

 a. What happens in these verses?

 b. Now read Mark 9:1–32. Name three things that happen in this passage.

 Argument re: The best

 c. In looking at the context, what surprises you about the disciples' discussion about greatness?

 d. Write your most honest reaction to Jesus' statement "If anyone would be first, he must be last of all and servant of all" (Mark 9:35).

 e. What does Jesus do after He says this?

 f. In a parallel passage, Jesus says, "Truly, I say to you, unless you turn and become like children, you will never enter the kingdom of heaven. Whoever humbles himself like this child is the greatest in the kingdom of heaven" (Matthew 18:3–4). What qualities do children have that contribute to greatness in God's upside-down kingdom?

2. Read John 3:22–36.

    a. What is happening in these verses?

    b. What are John the Baptist's disciples concerned about (v. 26)?

    c. How does John the Baptist describe himself (v. 29)?

    d. Based on John the Baptist's words, how would you describe his emotions at what was happening? Circle any of the feelings below that you think apply to John the Baptist at this time. Then imagine what you would have felt if you had been in his place. Put a box around the feelings you might have experienced. Explain your answers.

    Angry _____

    Joyful _____

    Disappointed _____

    Hopeful _____

    Jealous _____

    Fulfilled _____

    e. Record the words of John 3:30 and then write how your life might look if you had the same attitude.

3. Read Luke 18:9–14.

    a. Looking at the Pharisee's prayer, describe how he views God.

    b. How does the tax collector view God?

    c. Which man was approved by God? What does this tell you about God?

    d. Write a prayer thanking God for His mercy and grace and that we don't have to find our worth in being good enough.

Cultivate Enough

1. What "Un-" labels have you worn? "Unacceptable"? "Unacknowledged"? "Unattractive"? "Unwanted"? "Unimportant"? "Unlovable"? List some of the negative labels you have given yourself when you feel you are not enough.

Now look up some of the following verses and write the labels God gives you.

    Psalm 18:19

    Psalm 139:14

✓ Song of Solomon 4:7 — *perfect / beautiful*

Isaiah 43:4 — *Precious, valuable*

Isaiah 61:10 — *Salvation, righteous*

Jeremiah 29:12 — *God listens to us.*

Jeremiah 31:3 — *loving kindness*

Ezekiel 36:25 — *purity*

Nahum 1:7 — *safe*

Ephesians 1:4 — *holy, Chosen*

Make yourself a name tag with the label from God's Word that means the most to you today. If you are doing this study in a group, hand out name tags and have everyone put their favorite God-given label on the tag. Share with one another what this label means to you and how it erases the "Un-" labels you've been wearing.

Don't be surprised if the feeling of enough in Christ or the erasure of your "Un-" label doesn't last—feelings often don't. That's why we need to go back to the reality of God baptizing us into Christ, receiving His real body and blood, reading His life-giving words again and again. When we see Him face-to-face in heaven, the erasure of our "Un-" label will be perfectly complete and will last forever.

2. Worship the God of sufficiency with a song from your heart. Some ideas include "Who You Say I Am" by Hillsong, "What Love Is This" by Kari Jobe, "Just as I Am, without One Plea" (*LSB* 570), and "Baptized into Your Name Most Holy" (*LSB* 590).

CHAPTER 8 **ENOUGH FOR NOW** STUDY QUESTIONS

Reflect on the Reading

1. Think back to a time when you received something you had desired for a long time. How long did your satisfaction last? Write about the experience.

2. Give your reaction to this quote from Augustine: "The whole life of a good Christian is a holy longing." In this chapter, we talked about living with the realization that this world cannot truly satisfy, but that God will ultimately give us more than we can imagine. Circle the concepts we discussed that are most helpful to you to live with "enough for now."

> Worship the God of sufficiency.
>
> Look forward to goodness.
>
> Give God your list.
>
> Experience "enough for now" moments.
>
> Live with anticipation.
>
> Live unsatisfied.

Why did you circle those?

Dig into Scripture

Use the verse-mapping technique to dig into Luke 12:30–31. Look back at pages 148–49 for instructions on this Bible study method.

VERSE MAPPING: **LUKE 12:30–31**

Write out these verses from your favorite translation of the Bible.
Highlight important words.

Context: What is happening before and after these verses?

Other versions: Look up Luke 12:30–31 in different translations. Write out your favorites here.

Cross-references: What other Scripture passages are related to these verses?

Choose some of the words you highlighted in Luke 12:30–31. Write them here, then look them up in a Greek and/or English dictionary.

Paraphrase: Write out the verses in your own words, using what you have learned.

Apply the Word to Your Life

1. Read the parable of the rich fool in Luke 12:13–21 one more time. How might Jesus change the details of the story if He were directing it at you? What do you tend to accumulate or store? How would He get your attention? Write the story as you imagine Jesus telling the parable if you were in the crowd.

2. Read Isaiah 55—a mini textbook on living with "enough for now."

   a. God is speaking in this chapter. Is He addressing people who are content or people struggling with satisfaction? How can you tell (v. 1)?

   b. How are the people trying to satisfy their desires (v. 2)?

c. How have you done the same? What have you worked for or bought in an attempt to boost your happiness?

d. God gives the people better ideas for finding satisfaction. Write the solutions mentioned in these verses:

Verse 2b

Verse 3

Verse 6

Verse 7

e. The world can be a disappointing place. What truth about God's character can help us live with "enough for now" (vv. 8–9)?

f. On what can we base our hope, even when we don't understand what is happening now (vv. 10–11)?

g. One way we can experience "enough for now" is to live in anticipation. What does God promise for our future (vv. 12–13)?

h. What lesson from Isaiah 55 will help you live with "enough for now" today?

3. The writer of Hebrews told of the great heroes of faith who trusted God even though they didn't see the fulfillment of the promise of a Messiah. Their examples remind us we are "strangers and exiles" on earth, suffering homesickness for a home we have not yet experienced, but a home we know God is preparing for us. One way to live with "enough for now" is to live in anticipation of heaven. Read Revelation 21–22 and discover why our heavenly home is worth waiting for.

   a. What is the most wonderful thing about heaven (21:3; 22:4)?

   b. What is not present in heaven (21:4; 22:5)?

   c. Describe some of the physical characteristics of heaven (21:9–21).

   d. What gives heaven its light (21:22–25)?

   e. What is growing in heaven (22:1–2)? Why is this plant significant (Genesis 3:22–24)?

   f. How does knowing more about heaven help you live with "enough for now"?

Cultivate Enough

1. One of the best ways I know to cultivate enough in my life is to hunt down and capture "enough for now" moments. Although life is often disappointing, painful, and downright depressing, we have all received blessings from God. When we concentrate on those gifts, our unmet desires tend to fade into the background. Take some time to appreciate the goodness of God in your life through these simple exercises.

   "Enough for Now" Blessings in the Past: We all have experienced slivers of time when gratitude for the given has eclipsed any dissatisfaction we might feel. Think back to times when joy has filled your soul: a spectacular day on the beach, your wedding day, the births of your children, a worship service that drew you closer to God. Write down a few of these experiences.

   "Enough for Now" Blessings in the Present: Now pay attention to your everyday life and look for moments of joy and gratefulness right now: a bit of laughter shared with a friend, a perspective-altering book, a stunning sunset, a foamy salted-caramel latte, a precious promise in God's Word. Over the next few days, intentionally notice these "enough for now" moments and record them.

   "Enough for Now" Blessings in God's Word: It's easy to take God's gifts for granted. Hunt down some of the blessings God has already given us. Look up each verse and record the blessing mentioned.

"Enough for Now" Blessings

Blessings in the Past
Blessings in the Present

Blessings in God's Word

    Psalm 103:12

    John 3:16

    John 10:10

    John 14:27

    Romans 8:38–39

    Ephesians 1:13

Now make a copy of this list to remind you of all these blessings and post it where you will see it often.

2. Consider creating an "Enough for Now" collage. Find of photos of your "enough for now" moments in the past; print images of the things that give slivers of joy in the present; use your lettering skills or your computer to create beautiful renderings of the Scriptures listing God's blessings. Then paste them in an artful arrangement on poster board.

Display your collage where you will see it often. When discontentment shows up at your door, chase it away with a prayer of thanksgiving for some of the God-given gifts you have pictured.

3. Worship the God of sufficiency in song to remind you He is "enough for now." Try "Your Grace Is Enough" by Matt Maher, "Revelation Song" sung by Kari Jobe, "I'm But a Stranger Here" (*LSB* 748), or "Amazing Grace" (*LSB* 744).

CLOSING ACTIVITY

To review all you've learned in this study, fill out this simple chart. Look back in the study. Which Bible verses helped you the most in your journey to enough? What was the most important lesson you learned in each chapter?

Chapter	Scripture that spoke to my heart	Most important lesson I learned in living with "enough for now"
1. What Is Enough?		
2. Enough Money		
3. Enough Stuff		
4. Enough Food		
5. Enough Relationships		
6. Enough Time		
7. Enough of Me		
8. Enough for Now		

PARTING THOUGHTS

This world often seems like one big disappointment. We strive and struggle for more money, more stuff, more friends—certain that's what it takes for happiness. But somehow it's never enough. That's because enough can't be found here on earth—we can find it only in the God of sufficiency. He knew we could never be enough on our own, so He sent His Son into the world to save us. He outlined His wonderful plan of salvation in His Word:

"For all have sinned and fall short of the glory of God" (Romans 3:23). No one is perfect. Everyone fails to meet God's standard of sinlessness. This sin prevents us from coming to Him and from entering heaven.

"For God so loved the world, that He gave His only Son, that whoever believes in Him should not perish but have eternal life" (John 3:16). God loved us so much that He sent His own Son to take the punishment we deserved for our sins and mistakes. Jesus' death enables us to live with God—forever.

"For by grace you have been saved through faith. And this is not your own doing; it is the gift of God" (Ephesians 2:8). God gives us faith to believe in Jesus. His grace and mercy save us from death.

"But to all who did receive Him, who believed in His name, He gave the right to become children of God" (John 1:12). By receiving Jesus in the waters of Baptism and the Holy Word of God, we become part of God's family.

I invite you to pray this prayer to the God who loves you and wants you to be part of His family:

Father in heaven, I realize that I am a sinner and fall short of what You want for my life. I know that I cannot save myself or earn eternal life. Thank You for sending Your Son, Jesus, to die for me. Through the power of His resurrection, You have made me alive eternally. Help me to turn from my sins and follow You. Thank You that although I will still fail, You will forgive me because Jesus paid the price for my sins. Thank You for Your gift of faith in Jesus, my Savior, and for the promise of eternal life with You. In Jesus' name I pray. Amen.

God speaks His words of love and grace to you. Through God's free gift of faith in Jesus, you now are part of God's family!

ACKNOWLEDGMENTS

Writing this book has been a spiritual journey, one that culminated in greater personal contentment. But I could not have done it alone. I wish to thank:

God: I have always lived as if satisfaction was just out of reach. But in the process of writing this book, You have taught me that when I rest in Your sufficiency, I can find joy—even though this world may disappoint. You give me the grace to live with "enough for now."

John: Thanks for reading and rereading my words. For offering helpful suggestions and life-renewing support. For modeling what it means to live with "enough for now."

Family: To Mom, Anna and Nate, Nathaniel and Mary, Steven and Theresa, Shelly and Dave, Kathy and Bob—you all make life much richer.

Writing friends: Afton Rorvik, Catherine McNiel, Aubrey Sampson, Mary Anderson, and Jan May—I appreciate your prayers, support, and invaluable wisdom in shaping this book.

Bible study gals: Pam Barrett, Rhonda McIntyre, Deb Morris, and Sue Scholz—thanks for once again taking one of my studies on its maiden voyage. Most of all, thank you for adding friendship and laughter to my Wednesday nights!

Concordia Publishing House: Thanks to all who worked so hard on the content, design, and marketing of this book. Melissa, your artistry makes this book shine! I owe a special thank you to Peggy Kuethe, editor extraordinaire, who took a chance on my first book and continues to shape and hone my words.

ANSWERS

Note: For the "Dig into Scripture" sections where individual words are examined, the English Standard Version of the Bible was used. Definitions were drawn from BlueLetterBible.org and Dictionary.com.

CHAPTER 1

Reflect on the Reading: 1. Answers will vary. 2. Synonyms for *enough*: sufficient, ample, bounteous, satisfying, abundance. 3. Answers will vary.

Dig into Scripture: Verse mapping: Luke 12:32. **Context:** Before this verse, Jesus tells the parable of the rich fool to emphasize the dangers of greed. After this verse, Jesus urges His followers to be ready for His return. **Other versions:** Answers will vary. **Cross-references:** Possible answers: Isaiah 40:11; Matthew 10:31; Matthew 7:7; Matthew 13:11–12. **Word meanings:** Possible answers: *Fear*— Greek *phobeō*: to fear, to be afraid; English: a distressing emotion caused by impending danger, whether real or imagined. *Good pleasure*—Greek *eudokeó*: to choose or determine, to do willingly, to be well pleased with; English: enjoyment or satisfaction. *Give*—Greek *didómi*: to give something of one's own accord, to bestow a gift; English: to give voluntarily without expecting anything in return. *Kingdom*—Greek *basileia*: kingship, dominion, rule, the territory belonging to a king, the blessings and benefits of God's heavenly kingdom; English: a realm or sphere of independent control. **Paraphrase:** Answers will vary but may include something like this: Don't be afraid. You are like little sheep who don't know what they need. But your heavenly Father knows exactly what you need, and it makes Him happy to give you blessings from His eternal kingdom.

Apply the Word to Your Life: 1. a. Answers will vary. b. Answers will vary. c. The rich man thinks he will be happy and satisfied when he has "ample goods laid up for many years" (v. 19). d. Answers will vary. 2. a. Answers will vary. b. We are anxious when we think we don't have enough. The rich man was anxious even when he had too much, wondering where to put it. c. The Father knows what we need. d. Answers will vary. e. Answers will vary.

Cultivate Enough: Answers will vary.

CHAPTER 2

Reflect on the Reading: Answers will vary.

Dig into Scripture: Verse mapping: Luke 12:33–34. **Context:** Before these verses, Jesus tells the parable of the rich fool to emphasize the dangers of greed. After these verses, Jesus urges His followers to be ready for His return. **Other versions:** Answers will vary. **Cross-references:** Possible answers: Matthew 19:21; Matthew 6:20; 1 Peter 1:3–4. **Word meanings:** Possible answers: *Possessions*—Greek *hyparchō*: wealth, property, things one possesses; English: property, wealth, ownership. *Grow old*—Greek *palaioó*: to become old, to decay, to become obsolete; English: to age. *Treasure*—Greek *thésauros*: good and precious things that are collected and stored; English: riches or wealth that are stored. *Heart*—Greek *kardia*: the center of physical and spiritual life, the seat of emotions and desires; English: the center of personality, especially of feelings. **Paraphrase:** Possible answer: Sell your wealth and property and give to the needy. Seek out purses that don't wear out, and collect good and precious things that cannot be taken away or ruined. Wherever your wealth is, there will be your feelings and emotions.

Apply the Word to Your Life: 1. a. He thought that if he laid up enough grain and goods, then he could relax and enjoy life. b. He could have shared his abundance. He could have kept the barns he already had and stored the surplus in temporary silos, but he chose to tear down his barns and build bigger ones—larger barns that would display his wealth and significance. c. Jesus said he was not rich toward God. He had accumulated temporary material wealth, but he had not given a thought to eternal, true riches. d. Answers will vary. e. Answers will vary. 2. a. Answers will vary. b. Answers will vary, but may include the following: trusting God for daily needs; saving for retirement and for emergencies but willingly sharing when we receive more than we need; sponsoring a child in a third-world country; giving to missionaries and charities. c. We are to realize that "we brought nothing into the world, and we cannot take anything out of the world" (1 Timothy 6:7) and understand "the uncertainty of riches" (v. 17). We are to remember that the love of money can actually be risky, leading us "into temptation, into a snare, into many senseless and harmful desires that plunge people into ruin and destruction" (v. 9). d. Paul charges the rich "not to be haughty," remembering that God is the source of everything we own (v. 17). e. Paul advises the rich in this world to be generous and ready to share. Giving away our earthly treasure is the way to store up true treasure (vv. 18–19).

Cultivate Enough: Answers will vary.

CHAPTER 3

Reflect on the Reading: Answers will vary.

Dig into Scripture: Verse mapping: Luke 12:15. **Context:** Jesus said this after a man asked Him to tell his brother to divide an inheritance with him. Jesus continues to teach on greed by telling the parable of the rich fool. **Other versions:** Answers will vary. **Cross-references:** Answers will vary but might include Job 20:20 and Psalm 62:10. **Word meanings:** Possible answers: *Take care*—Greek *horaó*: to see, with eyes or mind, to take heed, beware; English: beware; to be wary, cautious, or careful of. *Covetousness*—Greek *pleonexia*: greedy desire to have more, avarice; English: greed; an excessive desire for wealth or possessions. *Abundance*—Greek *perisseuó*: to abound, overflow; English: an extremely plentiful or oversufficient quantity or supply. *Possessions*—Greek *hyparchō*: property, goods, things one has; English: ownership, property, or wealth. **Paraphrase:** Answers will vary. Possible answer: Beware! For your own safety, avoid greed and covetousness. Be careful to note excessive desire for wealth or possessions. Real, genuine life is not defined by an overflowing amount of possessions.

Apply the Word to Your Life: 1. a. Deuteronomy 10:14: Heaven and earth belong to God. 1 Chronicles 29:11–12: All that is in heaven and earth is the Lord's. Riches and honor come from God. Psalm 50:10–12: Cattle, birds, and beasts of the field all belong to God. The world and its fullness are His. b. Responses will vary. 2. a. We go to our possessions for happiness and self-worth. We make them more important than God, which makes them our idols. b. When we are discontent about out possessions or our situation in life, it can be difficult to offer thanks. But when we return to God and are thankful for what God has already given— eternal life and forgiveness of sins—the things we don't have seem much less important. 3. a. One bought a field. One bought five yoke of oxen. One got married. b. Answers will vary, but might include: The things we buy and own in this world may occupy so much of our time that we don't have time to spend with the One who gave us those possessions. Our earthly relationships may take priority over our spiritual life. c. The poor and crippled and blind and lame came. The ones who attended were those who did not own much. We must remember that we are all beggars in God's kingdom. We must guard against letting our earthly possessions get in the way of participating in a rich relationship with God.

Cultivate Enough: Answers will vary.

CHAPTER 4

Reflect on the Reading: Answers will vary.

Dig into Scripture: Verse mapping: Luke 12:29. **Context:** Before this verse, Jesus tells the parable of the rich fool. After the verse, He talks about being ready for His second coming. **Other versions:** Answers will vary. **Cross-references:** Answers will vary but might include Luke 12:22; Matthew 6:31; Philippians 4:6; Jeremiah 17:8. **Word meanings:** Possible answers: *Seek*—Greek *zēteō*: to seek after, seek for, aim at, strive after; English: to go in search of or try to obtain. *Eat*—Greek *phago*: to eat, to take food; English: to take into the mouth and consume for nourishment. *Drink*—Greek *pinó*: to drink; English: to take water or other liquid into the mouth and swallow it. *Worried*—Greek *meteórizomai*: to agitate or make anxious, from the metaphor of a ship tossed on high seas; English: to torment oneself with disturbing thoughts. **Paraphrase:** Possible answer: God asks us not to strive after what we are to eat or drink. We are not to be agitated by these disturbing thoughts.

Apply the Word to Your Life: 1. Answers will vary. 2. a. Psalm 71:19: God is righteous. Proverbs 21:21: When we pursue righteousness, we will find life and honor. Romans 3:21–22: The righteousness of God is available to all who believe in Jesus Christ. Romans 4:5: Righteousness does not come from trying to earn salvation but through faith and trust in Jesus. Ephesians 6:14: Righteousness is one of our spiritual weapons. b. Hungering and thirsting after righteousness doesn't mean trying to be perfect, but to seek God, to trust in God's goodness, and to rest in Jesus' saving work on the cross. Practically speaking, it will look like a desire to know God better and grow in faith. A yearning for righteousness can curb unhealthy cravings because as we grow in faith, we accept God's blessings and trust Him to give us other desires as He sees fit. We rest in our state of being made right with God and therefore can resist the temptation to make ourselves feel better through food or money or status. 3. Answers will vary.

Cultivate Enough: Answers will vary.

CHAPTER 5

Reflect on the Reading: Answers will vary.

Dig into Scripture: Verse mapping: 1 John 4:7. **Context:** Before this verse, John urges his readers to beware of false prophets—to test every spirit to see if it is from God. After this verse, John continues to teach about God's love and our love for others. **Other versions:** Answers will vary. **Cross-references:** Answers will vary but could include 1 John 3:11; John 13:34–35; John 15:12. **Word meanings:** Possible answers: *Beloved*—Greek *agapétos*: beloved, esteemed, dear, favorite, worthy of love; English: greatly loved, dear to the heart. *Love*—Greek *agapaé*: to welcome, to entertain, to be fond of, to love dearly. In Greek, there are four words for love. Agape love is the highest form of love—a love of the will, a love that has no limits, a selfless love. English: a profoundly tender, passionate affection for another person. *Born*—Greek *gennaé*: of God making people His children through faith in Christ's work; English: brought forth by birth. *Knows*—Greek *ginóskó*: to learn to know, come to know, perceive, feel; English: be acquainted with (a thing, place, person), as by sight, experience, or report. **Paraphrase:** Possible answer: God loves us—we are precious in His eyes. Therefore we should have selfless agape love for one another. We receive this love from God and give it to the people in our lives. Doing this demonstrates that we have come to know God personally and are part of His family.

Apply the Word to Your Life: 1. a. He wanted Jesus to tell his brother to divide the family inheritance with him. b. Jesus is judge, but a judge of spiritual matters. He did not want to settle civil disputes. Instead, He wanted to draw the man's attention to more significant matters—his spiritual life and the importance of being rich toward God instead of being rich in money. c. Answers will vary. d. Answers will vary. 2. a. Answers will vary, but might include: Working for riches never satisfies, but there is great wealth in supportive relationships. b. Answers might include working extra-long hours instead of spending time with family; putting a lot of effort into acquiring new things while ignoring friends in need; finding our worth in the size of our bank account instead of the wealth of friends. c. Answers will vary. 3. a. God always listens. b. God is our husband. c. God is my friend. d. God knows me. e. God chose me. f. God is my Father.

Cultivate Enough: Answers will vary.

CHAPTER 6

Reflect on the Reading: Answers will vary.

Dig into Scripture: Verse mapping: Luke 12:25–26. **Context:** Before this verse, Jesus instructs us not to be anxious about our lives. After this verse, He tells us to seek God's kingdom. **Other versions:** Answers will vary. **Cross-references:** Answers will vary, but might include Psalm 39:5; Psalm 144:4; Ecclesiastes 6:12. **Word meanings:** Possible answers: *Anxious*—Greek *merimnaó*: to worry or be troubled with cares; English: to suffer from distressing thoughts, to fret. *Add*—Greek *prostithémi*: add or increase; English: to unite so as to increase the quantity, importance, or size. *Span of life*—Greek *hélikia*: age, length of life; English: the longevity of an individual. *Small*—Greek *elachistos*: what is smallest or least in size, amount, or importance; English: of limited size, not great in amount, degree, extent, duration, value. **Paraphrase:** Possible answer: We cannot worry ourselves into a longer life span—no amount of anxiety will add to the length of our existence on earth. We cannot even do this small, insignificant thing, so why worry at all?

Apply the Word to Your Life: 1. a. Job 36:26: We cannot know the number of God's years. Isaiah 51:6: The earth will wear out like a piece of clothing, but God's salvation and righteousness last forever. 2 Peter 3:8: To God a day is like a thousand years and a thousand years like one day. Revelation 1:8: God is the beginning and the end. He is, and was, and is to come. b. The psalm describes our lifetimes as a few handbreadths, a mere breath, nothing. Answers will vary on the other questions. c. Answers will vary. 3. a. He tells us not to be anxious about tomorrow. Anxiety can't add even an hour to our lives. b. Answers will vary but might include: Anxiety over what might happen tomorrow could cause us to miss simple beauties today. Worry about getting everything done before a future deadline might make us too stressed to work effectively. Waiting until everything is "perfect" can cause us to miss what is good right now. c. We can rejoice in God, remembering that our trials are for a little while. We can love God and believe His Word, even though we cannot see Him now. 4. a. *Kairos* can mean a season—the right time for fruit. b. *Kairos* can mean the proper time to do something. c. *Kairos* can refer to a specific time for something. After we have repented, God blots out our sins and gives us times of renewal. d. *Kairos* can mean an opportunity, the right time to do something. Answers to the last part of the question will vary.

Cultivate Enough: Answers will vary.

CHAPTER 7

Reflect on the Reading: Answers will vary.

Dig into Scripture: Verse mapping: Luke 12:24. **Context:** Before this verse, Jesus tells His followers not to worry about what they will eat or drink. After this verse, He reminds them of the Father's care. **Other versions:** Answers will vary. **Cross-references:** Answers will vary but might include Isaiah 43:4; Matthew 6:26; Matthew 10:29–31. **Word meanings:** *Consider*—Greek *katanoeó*: to consider attentively, to focus on; English: to think carefully about. *Storehouse*—Greek *tameion*: a storage chamber; English: a place for storage. *Feeds*—Greek *trephó*: to nourish, support, nurture; English: to supply with nourishment. *More valuable*—Greek *diapheró*: to surpass, be more excellent, be of more value; English: having monetary worth or having qualities worthy of esteem and respect. **Paraphrase:** Think carefully about the birds. They don't store up goods; they don't even have barns or storerooms. But God constantly feeds and nourishes them. He will also take care of you; you are much more precious and valuable to Him than birds.

Apply the Word to Your Life: 1. a. The disciples argued with one another about who was greatest. b. (1) Jesus was transfigured, appearing in radiant glory, and Moses and Elijah appeared with Him. (2) Jesus cast out a demon that the disciples could not. (3) Jesus talked about His death and resurrection. c. Answers will vary but might include the following: How could the disciples argue about their own greatness after they witnessed Jesus' glory and His power over demons? How could they be concerned with their own petty reputations when Jesus had just talked about dying? d. Answers will vary. e. Jesus calls a child into their midst and tells the disciples that whoever receives such a child receives Him. f. Answers will vary, but might include humility, innocence, trusting hearts, meekness. 2. a. John the Baptist is baptizing people and John's disciples tell him that Jesus is also baptizing nearby. b. They are concerned that more people are going to Jesus than to John. c. He describes himself as the friend of the Bridegroom. He realizes that he is not the focal point; Jesus is. d. Answers will vary. e. Answers will vary. 3. a. The Pharisee views God as someone who judges according to good deeds and generous giving. He thinks he needs to impress God. b. The tax collector views God as merciful and as one who gives grace when we admit our need for it. c. The tax collector was approved by God. This demonstrates that God does not give grace and mercy because we deserve it or as a result of earning it; He gives it freely as we humble ourselves before Him. d. Answers will vary.

Cultivate Enough: Psalm 18:19: rescued, delighted in; Psalm 139:14: fearfully and wonderfully made; Song of Solomon 4:7: beautiful; Isaiah 43:4: precious, honored; Isaiah 61:10: clothed in salvation and covered in righteousness; Jeremiah 29:12: heard; Jeremiah 31:3: loved; Ezekiel 36:25: clean; Nahum 1:7: known; Ephesians 1:4: chosen, holy, blameless.

CHAPTER 8

Reflect on the Reading: Answers will vary.

Dig into Scripture: Verse mapping: Luke 12:30–31. **Context:** Before these verses, Jesus tells us not to worry. After these verses, Jesus reminds us that the Father is pleased to give us His kingdom. **Other versions:** Answers will vary. **Cross-references:** Answers will vary but might include Matthew 6:8; Matthew 5:6; Matthew 25:34; John 3:3, 5; Matthew 7:11. **Word meanings:** *Seek* (v. 30)—Greek *epizéteó*: to search for diligently, to crave, to demand; English: to go in search of or try to obtain. *World*—Greek *kosmos*: the inhabitants of the world, the people alienated from God; English: the earth with its inhabitants. *Seek* (v. 31)—Greek *zēteō*: to seek in order to find, to strive after; English: to go in search or quest of, to try to obtain. In the Bible, *zēteō* is used for seeking God, while *epizéteó* is used for seeking things. *Kingdom*—Greek *basileia*: the royal power and dignity conferred on Christians in the Messiah's kingdom; English: the spiritual sovereignty of God or Christ and the domain over which the spiritual sovereignty of God or Christ extends, whether in heaven or on earth. **Paraphrase:** The people who don't know God diligently search for and crave food and clothing and the things of this world, but you don't have to because your heavenly Father sees your needs. Instead, seek for and strive after God's kingdom—the spiritual place where God rules and where Christians have royal power and dignity because of Christ. Then the other things you need will also be given to you.

Apply the Word to Your Life: 1. Answers will vary. 2. a. God is addressing people struggling with satisfaction. Verse 1 calls out to the people who are thirsty and hungry and broke. b. They are working for and buying things they think will satisfy them. c. Answers will vary. d. Verse 2b: Find delight in God's rich blessings. Verse 3: Listen to God and go to Him. Verse 6: Seek God. Verse 7: Return to the Lord and receive forgiveness. e. God's thoughts and ways are so far above our own that we can't understand everything that is happening. He has an eternal perspective. Although circumstances may look bleak to us, God sees how they fit together for good. f. God's Word—it will never disappoint. It will always accomplish what God intends. g. He promises joy and peace. He promises abundant life, symbolized by the cypress and myrtle, instead of pain and heartache, symbolized by the thorn and brier. h. Answers will vary. 3. a. God will dwell with us. We will be His people and He will be our God. We will see Him face-to-face. b. There won't be tears, death, mourning, crying, pain, or night. c. The new Jerusalem will appear with the radiance of a rare jewel. The city will measure about 1,380 miles in each direction and will be made of pure gold. Each gate in the wall will be made of a different jewel. d. The glory of God will light heaven, and the Lamb of God will be its lamp. e. The tree of life is growing in heaven. The tree of life was in the Garden of Eden, but after sin entered the world, God removed Adam and Eve from the garden so they would not have access to the tree of life and live forever in sin. In heaven, because of Christ's work on a different kind of tree, we will again be able to enjoy the fruit and live eternally. f. Answers will vary.

Cultivate Enough: "'Enough for Now' Blessings in the Past": Answers will vary. "'Enough for Now' Blessings in the Present": Answers will vary. "'Enough for Now' Blessings in God's Word": Psalm 103:12: forgiveness of sins; John 3:16: eternal life; John 10:10: abundant life; John 14:27: peace; Romans 8:38–39: God's love; Ephesians 1:13: the Holy Spirit. 2.–3. Answers will vary.

CLOSING ACTIVITY

Answers will vary.

NOTES

Chapter 1

1   See Claire Gordon, "Unhappy at Work? A Wantologist Will Help, for $200 an Hour," *Huffington Post*, July 19, 2012, www.huffingtonpost.com/2012/07/18/unhappy-at-work-a-wantologist-will-help_n_1680435.html.

2   Arthur W. Klinck and Erich H. Kiehl, *Everyday Life in Bible Times* (St. Louis: Concordia Publishing House, 1982), 30–47.

3   Augustine, *The Confessions of St. Augustine: Modern English Version* (Grand Rapids, MI: Baker Book House, 2005), Kindle.

4   Luther's Small Catechism, Ninth Commandment.

5   Augustine, *The Confessions of St. Augustine*, Kindle.

6   Jen Pollock Michel, *Teach Us to Want: Longing, Ambition, and the Life of Faith* (Downers Grove, IL: InterVarsity Press, 2014), 84.

7   Michel, *Teach Us to Want*, 38.

8   *Lutheran Bible Companion*, vol. 2 (St. Louis: Concordia Publishing House, 2014), 291.

9   Augustine, *The Confessions of St. Augustine*, Kindle.

10 Caryn Dahlstrand Rivadeneira, *Grumble Hallelujah: Learning to Love Your Life Even When It Lets You Down* (Carol Stream, IL: Tyndale Publishers, 2011), 180.

Chapter 2

1   David Futrelle, "Here's How Money Really Can Buy You Happiness," *Time*, time.com/collection/guide-to-happiness/4856954/can-money-buy-you-happiness.

2   Robert Frank, "What Does It Take to Feel Wealthy?" *CNBC*, July 19, 2012, www.cnbc.com/id/48240956.

3   Randy Alcorn, *Money, Possessions, and Eternity* (Carol Stream, IL: Tyndale Publishers, 2003), Kindle.

4   Luther's Large Catechism I 7–8, *Concordia: The Lutheran Confessions*, second edition (St. Louis: Concordia Publishing House, 2006), 358.

5   Questions adapted from Alcorn, *Money, Possessions, and Eternity*, Kindle.

6   R. C. H. Lenski, *The Interpretation of St. Luke's Gospel* (Minneapolis: Augsburg Publishing House, 1946, 1961), 692.

7   aaifp.ejoinme.org/MyPates/DonationPage/tabid/204189/Default.aspx.

8   Thanks to social worker Matthew McNiel for these ideas.

9   Martin Luther, quoted at www.brainyquote.com/quotes/martin_luther390009.html.

Chapter 3

1   Benjamin Franklin, www.bartleby.com/349/authors/77.html.

2   Christian Jarrett, "Why Are We So Attached to Our Things?" *TedEd*, ed.ted.com/lessons/why-are-we-so-attached-to-our-things-christian-jarrett.

3   "Manners & Customs: Grain," *Bible History Online*, www.bible-history.com/links.php?cat=39&sub=773&cat_name=Manners+%26+Customs&subcat_name=Grain.

4   Charles Haddon Spurgeon Quotes, www.goodreads.com/quotes/189188-you-say-if-i-had-a-little-more-i-should.

5   Joshua Becker, *Simplify: 7 Guiding Principles to Help Anyone Declutter Their Home and Life* (© 2010, Joshua Becker), Kindle.

6   Matthew Henry, "Commentary on Luke 12," www.blueletterbible.org/Comm/mhc/Luk/Luk_012. cfm?a=985001.

7   Amanda Gardner, "12 Ways We Sabotage Our Mental Health," *Health*, November 2, 2015, www.health. com/health/gallery/0,,20694928,00.html#ignoring-clutter-0.

8   Mikael Cho, "How Clutter Affects Your Brain (and What You Can Do about It), *Lifehacker*, July 5, 2013, lifehacker.com/how-clutter-affects-your-brain-and-what-you-can-do-abo-662647035.

9   Audrey Sherman, "The Link between Disorganization, Depression, and Anxiety," *Psych Central*, June 21, 2016, blogs.psychcentral.com/dysfunction/2016/06/the-link-between-disorganization-depression-and-anxiety/.

10   Joshua Becker, "'Does It Spark Joy?' Is the Wrong Decluttering Question," *Becoming Minimalist*, www. becomingminimalist.com/does-it-spark-joy-is-the-wrong-decluttering-question/.

11   *Luther's Small Catechism with Explanation*, Question 90.

12   *Luther's Small Catechism with Explanation*, Question 91.

13   *Luther's Small Catechism with Explanation*, Question 92.

Chapter 4

1   "*Zaō*," KJV Blue Letter Bible, www.blueletterbible.org/lang/lexicon/lexicon.cfm?Strongs=G2198&t=KJV.

2   Spiros Zodhiates, ThD, *The Complete Word Study Dictionary New Testament* (Chattanooga, TN: AMG Publishers, 1992), 700–701.

3   *Baby Blues*, February 20, 2014, babyblues.com/comics/february-20-2014/.

4   Klinck and Kiehl, *Everyday Life in Bible Times*, 64–81.

5   Lee Wolfe Blum, *Table in the Darkness: A Healing Journey through an Eating Disorder* (Downer's Grove, IL: InterVarsity Press, 2013), Kindle.

6   Paul E. Kretzmann, *Popular Commentary of the Bible New Testament, Vol. 1* (St. Louis: Concordia Publishing House 1924), 443.

7   *Luther's Small Catechism with Explanation*, 335.

8   *Luther's Small Catechism with Explanation*, Question 366.

Chapter 5

1   Stephanie Pappas, "7 Ways Friendships Are Good for Your Health," *LiveScience*, January 8, 2016, www. livescience.com/53315-how-friendships-are-good-for-your-health.html.

2   Adapted from Ruth Soukup, *Unstuffed: Decluttering Your Home, Mind, and Soul* (Grand Rapids, MI: Zondervan, 2016), 169–70.

3   Klinck and Kiehl, *Everyday Life in Bible Times*, 163–64.

Chapter 6

1   Amy Greer, "Notes from a Musician's Journal," *American Music Teacher*, October/November 2008, 14.

2   Klinck and Kiehl, *Everyday Life in Bible Times*, 140–41.

3   Charles Pope, "How Did People Tell Time in Jesus' Day?" *Community in Mission*, August 11, 2014, blog. adw.org/2014/08/how-did-people-tell-time-in-jesus-time/.

4   "The Biblical Feast Days—God's Calendar," biblelight.net/feasts.htm.

5   William J. Bennett, *The Book of Virtues* (New York: Simon & Schuster, 1993), 57–63.

6   "*Exagorazō*," KJV Blue Letter Bible, www.blueletterbible.org/lang/lexicon/lexicon. cfm?Strongs=G1805&t=KJV.

7   "*Exagorazō*," KJV Blue Letter Bible

8   W. E. Vine, Merrill F. Unger, William White Jr., *Vine's Complete Expository Dictionary of Old and New Testament Words* (Nashville: Thomas Nelson Publishers, 1985), 554.

9   Matthew Henry, "Commentary on Ephesians 5," www.blueletterbible.org/Comm/mhc/Eph/Eph_005. cfm?a=1102016.

10 See John 5:30; 6:38; 8:26; 9:4; 10:37–38; 12:49–50; 14:31; 15:10; 17:4.

11 Dietrich Bonhoeffer, *Life Together: The Classic Exploration of Christian Community*, quoted at www. goodreads.com/work/quotes/168889-gemeinsames-leben

12 Richard Swenson, *Margin: Restoring Emotional, Physical, Financial, and Time Reserves to Overloaded Lives*, quoted at www.richardswenson.com/margin/.

Chapter 7

1   Larry Kim, "Yes, There Is a Key to Happiness (and It's Actually Pretty Simple)" *Inc.*, June 6, 2016, www.inc.com/larry-kim/yes-theres-a-key-to-happiness-and-its-actually-pretty-simple.html.

2   "$9.9 Billion Self-Improvement Market Challenged By Younger and More Demanding Millennials, Changing Technology," *Webwire*, August 2, 2017, www.webwire.com/ViewPressRel.asp?aId=211649.

3   Holley Gerth, *Fiercehearted: Live Fully, Love Bravely* (Grand Rapids, MI: Revell, 2017), 69.

4   From my notes from Dr. Reed Lessing's Bible study at the Lutheran Women's Missionary League Convention in Peoria, Ill., June 24, 2011.

5   "Like a Pro: Anthem Courtesy of GMC," Sunset Chevrolet Buick GMC, June 8, 2017, www.youtube.com/watch?v=oY5R-I10E5g.

6   Oswald Chambers, "Impulivesness or Discipleship?" utmost.org/impulsiveness-or-discipleship.

7   *The Lutheran Study Bible*, 1557.

8   "The Rules of the Pharisees," www.pursuegod.org/rules-pharisees.

9   *The Lutheran Study Bible*, 1659.

10 *The Lutheran Study Bible*, 1589.

Chapter 8

1   Melody Wilding, "Why Reaching Your Goals Can Surprisingly Make You Less Happy," *Forbes*, August 22, 2016, www.forbes.com/sites/melodywilding/2016/08/22/why-reaching-your-goals-can-surprisingly-make-you-less-happy/#587429d1b880.

2   Heidi Grant Halvorson, "How To Keep Happiness From Fading," *Psychology Today*, August 15, 2012, www.psychologytoday.com/us/blog/the-science-success/201208/how-keep-happiness-fading.

3   John Burnaby, ed., *Augustine: Later Works* (Philadelphia: The Westminster Press, 1955), 290.

4   Thomas à Kempis, quoted in "Worship—The Heart's Healer," *Ransomed Heart*, August 25, 2016, www.ransomedheart.com/daily-reading/worship%E2%80%94-heart%E2%80%99s-healer.

5   Carla Herreria, "The Happiest Part Of Your Vacation Isn't What You Think," *Huffington Post*, June 8, 2016, www.huffpost.com/entry/how-to-make-the-most-of-vacation_n_5755b42ae4b0eb20fa0e906d.

6   *Luther's Small Catechism with Explanation*, 258.

7   Amy Simpson, *Blessed Are the Unsatisfied* (Downers Grove, IL: InterVarsity Press, 2018), 41.

8   Simpson, *Blessed Are the Unsatisfied*, 41.

Study Guide

1   "*Dikaiosynē*," KJV Blue Letter Bible, www.blueletterbible.org/lang/lexicon/lexicon.cfm?Strongs=G1343&t=KJV